CW00456860

Reflections on Counselling

Dedication

*For Martin Cole – fearless pioneer in
sex therapy and good friend.*

Reflections on Counselling

Windy Dryden

Foreword by
Arnold A. Lazarus

Distinguished Professor, Rutgers University, New Jersey, USA

Whurr Publishers
London

© 1993 Windy Dryden

First published 1993 by
Whurr Publishers Ltd
19b Compton Terrace, London N1 2UN, England

All rights reserved. No part of this publication may be reproduced, stored in a retrieval system, or transmitted in any form or by any means, electronic, mechanical, photocopying, recording or otherwise, without the prior permission of Whurr Publishers Limited.

This publication is sold subject to the conditions that it shall not, by way of trade or otherwise, be lent, resold, hired out, or otherwise cir-culated without the publisher's prior consent in any form of binding or cover other than that in which it is published and without a similar condition including this condition being imposed upon any subsequent purchaser.

British Library Cataloguing in Publication Data
A catalogue record for this book is available from the
British Library.

ISBN 1-897635-10-9

Photoset by Stephen Cary
Printed and bound in the UK by Athenaeum Press Ltd,
Newcastle upon Tyne

Foreword

Professor Dryden sent me several of the essays that comprise *Reflections on Counselling* and asked for my reactions. I was so taken with them that I gave them to students in a seminar on issues in counselling and psychotherapy and asked for specific critiques. The upshot was an exceedingly stimulating discussion that generated so much debate and enthusiasm that I encouraged Professor Dryden to publish them in book form. When he informed me that he had taken my advice, found a publisher and asked for a foreword, I was delighted on all counts.

The thirty brief reflections that constitute the book address some of the most important aspects of the counselling process. My students found the many specific do's and don'ts invaluable, and they reacted most appreciatively to issues about relationship factors, directive and 'non-directive' approaches, the dangers of pejorative language and the significance of confidentiality.

This book underscores the need for clinical flexibility – a notion to which I have long been especially partial. Professor Dryden and I have shared our ideas about this concept and its therapeutic impact, and I was pleased to see that the importance of adopting what I have labelled the stance of a counsellor serving as an *authentic chameleon* has been introduced and explored.

Reflections on Counselling is a work that can only be written by someone with a wealth of experience. It is a book that draws from Dryden's academic and clinical prowess and succinctly underscores some truly poignant points and crucial strategies. For example, the matter of 'matchmaking' is one of the elements that Professor Dryden talks about in a humorous but telling fashion. While the formal literature on the therapeutic alliance and the necessity of establishing rapport have been addressed in many quarters, Dryden discusses the special 'chemistry' between counsellor and client, and the need to 'hit it off' with one another therapeutically, in a way that brings these weighty concepts down to earth. The fact that counsellors do not have to take on all referrals, but are at liberty to recommend more suitable resources, is a straightforward idea that comes as a surprise to many practitioners. However, once they reflect on this idea, they resonate to it readily, and indeed experience relief at being freed from an unfortunate imperative that is rife in our field.

Professor Dryden's experience as a long time counsellor educator, trainer and active clinician stands him in good stead to address current issues in this domain. Windy has neatly punctured a widespread belief that happens to be one of my pet peeves – that all counsellors and therapists *must* undergo personal therapy. He argues, quite rightly in my opinion, that while all practitioners should be concerned to develop themselves both personally and professionally, there is no one 'therapeutically correct' way of so doing. My own view is that if personal problems exist that undermine my trainees' effectiveness with their clients, personal therapy is often strongly recommended. If not, there are better, more useful and cost-effective avenues to traverse such as learning about oneself by attending experiential workshops, engaging in co-counselling relationships, and being in personal development groups with one's fellow trainees who can provide valuable feedback on one's interpersonal style.

I was especially pleased that Windy Dryden decided to include a section on personal experiences and reflections. Very often, leading figures in our field are only too willing to hide behind a professional façade, thus helping to perpetuate the myth of personal infallibility. Dryden's fitting and relevant self-disclosures not only humanise the book, but also provide an admirable model of how to integrate the personal, professional and the practical aspects of our field.

In short, I firmly believe that this book is one that practitioners and trainees will find easy to read and packed full of useful information.

Arnold A. Lazarus, PhD
Distinguished Professor, Graduate School of Applied and
Professional Psychology, Rutgers University, New Jersey, USA

Preface

In this book, I present thirty brief reflections on counselling.

These pieces are organised into seven sections. The first section, 'Counselling approaches and process', contains four pieces that consider general issues in the counselling process. The first two pieces aim to present my major personal counselling interests 'in a nutshell'. For most of my career I have been associated with cognitive–behavioural approaches to counselling and in the first piece I outline a thumbnail sketch of these approaches, focusing in particular on Beck's cognitive therapy and Ellis's rational–emotive therapy. The second piece reflects my continuing interest in therapeutic alliance theory. This theory states that counselling, from whatever tradition, can be viewed in terms of: (1) the interpersonal bonds that develop between counsellor and client; (2) the goals of the work; and (3) the tasks both counsellor and client engage in to further the achievement of these goals. The third piece addresses what I consider to be the myth of so-called 'non-directive' counselling, while the fourth piece considers whether or not rational–emotive therapists neglect the therapeutic relationship. The fifth piece is concerned with the use of audio tapes in counselling and supervision, a contentious issue, even though the practice was originated by none other than Carl Rogers.

The second section, 'Flexibility in counselling', reflects the influence that Arnold Lazarus has had on my thinking about counselling. The sixth piece takes as its starting point a chance and seemingly ordinary experience that I had on holiday – namely watching a moth trying to make good its escape through a closed window – and draws a parallel between this and the behaviour of many clients and counsellors in the counselling process. The seventh piece shows how reluctant many counsellors are to broaden their conceptual horizons, because in large part they prefer to remain comfortable within the confines of their restricted ideas. I argue that being uncomfortable, if this leads to greater flexibility in thought and practice, is productive for counsellors.

The next two pieces, which are linked, show how two traditional Jewish figures – shadchonim (or matchmakers) and bespoke tailors can serve as role models for good practice in counselling. Shadchonim (discussed in the eighth piece) can teach us the value of matching clients to counsellors, while bespoke tailors (discussed in the ninth piece) can teach us the value of masterful multimodal practice.

The third section, 'The semantics of counselling', demonstrates my interests in the use of language in counselling. In the tenth piece, I discuss three words commonly used by counsellors which I find quite irritating. I explain why in the piece. In the eleventh piece, I focus on the use of pejorative language which counsellors sometimes employ when referring to the work of their colleagues from different persuasions, while in the twelfth piece I discuss some of the misunderstandings people have of the words, 'rational' and 'irrational' as they are employed in rational–emotive therapy, an approach dear to my heart. In the final piece in this section, I discuss how clients frequently defeat themselves by waiting to feel confident, courageous and comfortable before they take constructive action.

In the fourth section, 'Ethical issues in counselling', I consider the ethics of carrying out research in counselling as exemplified in a study on the quality of counselling offered by telephone hotlines (piece 14) and the issue of confidentiality with respect to the care we need to take when discussing our work with clients in print (pieces 15 and 16), while, in piece 17, I discuss three ethical steps that newspapers need to take before advertising courses in counselling and psychotherapy.

In the fifth section, 'On clients', I discuss three memorable encounters with clients. The first concerns a dilemma I experienced with a client who kept threatening suicide (piece 18); the second describes an uncomfortable situation I found myself in with a client when I was forced to call the police (piece 19); while the third deals with an unusual encounter with a client outside the counselling room (piece 20).

In the sixth section, 'Counsellor education and training', I outline a number of issues which deal with that theme. In piece 21, I discuss whether there are differences between the terms, 'counsellor education' and 'counsellor training', while, in the following piece, I cast a doubtful eye over the trend towards training for counsellor trainers. In piece 23, I show how appraising research into counselling can be likened to an exercise in applied logic and how helping trainees to conceptualise it in this way encourages them to take a greater interest in that research; in piece 24, I consider the place of personal therapy in the training of counsellors and whether it should be mandatory or recommended. Finally, in piece 25, I provide a brief consumer's guide for those seeking counselling skills training.

In the seventh and final section, entitled 'Personal experiences and reflections', I introduce a more personal tone into my reflections, as the section title notes. Thus, in piece 26, I review some of my experiences while looking for employment after taking 'voluntary' redundancy from my post at Aston University. In piece 27, I present a dilemma I had concerning whether to continue publishing in the field – the existence of this book shows that I did resolve the dilemma! In the following piece, I lament the tendency for those in the field to pigeon-hole people and illustrate this tendency with some personal examples, while, in the penultimate piece, I describe what seems on the surface to be a mundane experience, but one which has a special place in my working life. Finally, to complete the book, I explain how I have used RET to overcome some of my emotional problems and reveal the origins of my name.

While this book may be used in many ways, it is particularly well suited for use on training courses. Each piece may usefully serve as a stimulus for discussion on the issue that the piece raises. My experience has been that the most fruitful exchange of views has been on a piece where the discussants have widely varying views about the relevant issue. Such is the diversity of views in the counselling and psychotherapy community that trainers will have little trouble in facilitating a useful discourse on the topics raised in these pieces. Indeed, if my experience is anything to go by, trainers may well have difficulty bringing the discussion to a close!

I have found the medium of the brief reflection to be one that I have taken to quite naturally. The discipline of writing economically is one that I can recommend to all aspiring writers on counselling. It encourages structure and hones one's ability to develop a theme briefly and with immediacy. I hope readers find the pieces contained herein instructive. If not, please let me know. I might even write another piece based on your replies!

Windy Dryden
London
February 1993

Acknowledgements

I wish to thank the British Association for Counselling, Central Magazine Ltd and Hobsons PLC for giving me permission to reproduce material here that was originally published in one of their publications.

Contents

Foreword   v
Preface   vi
Acknowledgements   x

Part I   Counselling approaches and process   1
1   Cognitive–behavioural approaches to counselling in a
         nutshell   2
2   The therapeutic alliance in a nutshell   4
3   W(h)ither non-directive counselling?   7
4   On neglecting the therapeutic relationship   10
5   To tape or not to tape? The use of audio tapes in
         counselling and supervision   13

Part II   Flexibility in counselling   19
6   If at first you don't succeed, stop fluttering your wings 20
7   The discomfort of being a counsellor   22
8   The counselling field needs shadchonim. . .   24
9   . . . and bespoke tailors too   27

Part III The semantics of counselling   31
10   Counselling, semantic precision and pedantry   32
11   Put-downs, insults and other disparaging remarks   35
12   The semantics of rationality   38
13   Putting the cart before the horse: the paradox of
         confidence, courage and comfort   41

Part IV   Ethical issues in counselling   45
14   Phony client, phony research   46
15   Confidentiality revisited   48
16   Counselling, disclosure and the press   50
17   On advertising courses in counselling and psychotherapy 53

Part V   On clients   **57**
18   Bound, but not gagged   58
19   Officer, my client won't leave   63
20   Oi Windy! Over here   66

Part VI Counsellor education and training   **69**
21   Counsellor training or counsellor education?   70
22   Training for the trainers of trainers of trainers . . ?   74
23   What does the label stand for? An exercise in applied logic   76
24   Personal therapy: mandatory or recommended?   80
25   A consumer's guide to counselling skills training   83

Part VII Personal experiences and reflections   **87**
26   Voluntary redundancy and beyond   88
27   Keep going, take a break or give up?   93
28   Specialists, all-rounders and pigeon-holes   95
29   Foodcourt for thought   97
30   A note on how I used RET to overcome my emotional
            problems   99

Index   **103**

Part I

Counselling approaches and process

1 Cognitive–behavioural approaches to counselling in a nutshell

Over the years I have received a number of requests to write a short piece describing, in a nutshell as it were, cognitive–behavioural approaches to counselling. I decided to put pen to paper when I was invited to prepare a short piece on these approaches for *The Seeker's Guide: A New Age Resource Book* edited by Button and Bloom.

As the name suggests, cognitive–behavioural approaches to counselling focus both on the way we think about ourselves, other people and the world, and on the way we act in the world. Contrary to what is often thought, however, these approaches do not neglect our emotions; rather, they stress that cognition (which includes thoughts, images and attitudes), behaviour and feelings are interdependent psychological processes.

While there are several different approaches within this area of counselling, two are best known in the UK: cognitive therapy and rational–emotive therapy. These two major approaches are similar in that counselling sessions tend to be structured and goal directed, the counsellor's style is that of an active–directive psychological educator, the therapeutic relationship is collaborative, the counsellor explains the rationale for his or her interventions and general approach, clients are encouraged to put their counselling-derived learning into practice between sessions, and clients are encouraged to become their own counsellors.

Cognitive therapy

Cognitive therapy, founded by Aaron Beck, is currently the most popular and widely practised approach in the cognitive–behavioural tradition. It was originally developed for use with depressed clients, but is now used more broadly, covering anxiety problems, relationship diffi-

First published in 1992.

culties and a wide range of so-called personality disorders.

In terms of therapeutic strategy, the counsellor first helps the client to identify, challenge and change dysfunctional 'automatic thoughts' (surface thoughts that pop into one's mind). This is called 'working at the level of cognitive events'. As counselling proceeds, greater emphasis is placed on working at the level of cognitive processes, where the counsellor and client investigate the latter's habitual style of faulty information processing in emotionally laden areas (a tendency to personalise, perhaps, or to magnify the importance of events). From there, counsellor and client work at the level of cognitive structures, changing underlying dysfunctional attitudes. A large variety of cognitive and behavioural techniques are employed in the service of these therapeutic aims.

Rational–emotive therapy

Rational–emotive therapy (RET) was founded by Albert Ellis in 1955 and is the oldest of the cognitive–behavioural approaches to counselling. It developed as a general approach to a wide variety of psychological difficulties, in contrast with the more specialised focus of cognitive therapy in the early period of its development.

Rational–emotive therapy differs from cognitive therapy in two main respects: first, the rational–emotive therapist proceeds much more quickly than a cognitive therapist in working at the level of dysfunctional cognitive structures (known in RET as irrational beliefs); secondly, while in cognitive therapy cognitive structures have no set form of expression, in RET irrational beliefs are deemed to occur in four distinct forms:

1. Dogmatic musts and shoulds (the goal of the counsellor is to help clients to stay with their healthy preferences and not to transmute these into absolute musts).
2. Grossly exaggerated evaluations (the goal is to help clients to evaluate negative events as 'bad', but not as 'terrible').
3. Low frustration tolerance (the goal is to encourage clients to raise their level of frustration tolerance as a way of coping better).
4. Damning self and others (the goal is to help clients to accept themselves and others as fallible human beings who cannot legitimately be given a single global rating).

As in cognitive therapy, a large variety of cognitive and behavioural methods are used in RET in the service of these therapeutic goals. However, more emphasis is placed on the use of emotive methods in RET than is the case in cognitive therapy.

2 The therapeutic alliance in a nutshell

Counsellors differ in their approach to counselling. While one estimate is that there are over 250 approaches to counselling, a more conservative position is that there are three main traditions in the field: psychodynamic, humanistic–existential and cognitive–behavioural. All three traditions acknowledge the importance of the relationship between counsellor and client, but there are substantial differences among them with respect to theory and practice. The *psychodynamic* approach attaches primary importance to early experience and unconscious processes; the *humanistic–existential* approach places emphasis on the creation of a particular 'climate' of relationship and on present feelings and experience; the *cognitive–behavioural* approach is primarily concerned with self-defeating thought and behaviour patterns and their amelioration. Although practitioners in these three traditions work in relative isolation from one another, recent developments in what has come to be known as 'therapeutic alliance theory' have provided counsellors with a way of communicating with one another which emphasises commonalities of approach and respects differences in working practices. What follows is a brief discussion of the concept of the therapeutic alliance.

Ed Bordin has put forward a tripartite conceptualisation of the therapeutic alliance in which he states that the alliance comprises *bonds, goals* and *tasks*. In short, and this is a view with which most, if not all, counsellors would concur, counselling is a process rooted in a *relationship* between the participants involved (bonds), has a *direction* (goals) and in which the participants have *work* to do (tasks).

I will consider each of these components in turn, but it must be stressed at the outset that in practice they frequently influence one another and should be regarded as interdependent factors.

First published in 1992.

Bonds

All counsellors would agree that the quality of the relationship between counsellor and client is important in determining the outcome of the work. Two major factors need to be taken into account when considering the quality of counselling relationships.

The first pertains to the presence or absence of certain counsellor core 'conditions'. In this respect research indicates a positive correlation between client outcome and the extent to which clients perceive their counsellors to be empathic, respectful and genuine.

The second 'bond' factor concerns the productive matching of interpersonal styles between counsellor and client. Different approaches to counselling advocate different styles of counsellor participation. Such styles vary along several important continua, for example active–passive, directive–non-directive, formal–informal, self-disclosing–non-self-disclosing. Effective counselling relationships are characterised by the productive fit between the interpersonal styles of counsellor and client rather than by any universally therapeutic counselling style. This means that within reason (and taking into account the limits of individual practitioners), effective counsellors vary their interpersonal style with different clients. For such 'matching' to be productive it has to be conducive to the *work* of counselling.

Goals

Counselling relationships frequently have a dual purpose: (1) to help relieve psychological distress; and (2) to promote healthy personal development. Counsellors differ in their views concerning both how a specific client's goals should be stated and how explicit to make the goal-setting process. However, effective counselling tends to occur when counsellor and client agree, explicitly or implicitly, about the goals of counselling and when these goals are conducive to the healthy development of the client. One way, then, that counselling can 'stall' is when counsellor and client have different ideas concerning the client's *goals* for change.

Tasks

If counselling is a purposeful activity, then it also places demands on both counsellor and client in that both have *tasks* to perform. Tasks are instrumental activities which both client and counsellor carry out to help one of them (the client) achieve his or her goals. I call these tasks 'change-related'. In this task component of the alliance the greatest differences are seen among different approaches to counselling.

Effective counselling, in the 'change-related' task domain of the alliance, is likely to occur when

1. Clients understand the nature of the counselling tasks that they are called upon to carry out.
2. Clients see the instrumental value of carrying out their tasks (i.e. doing so will help them to achieve their goals).
3. Clients have the ability and confidence to carry out the counselling tasks required of them (or are prepared to carry out these tasks unconfidently as a means of gaining such confidence – see pp. 41–43).
4. Clients see the nature of their counsellors' tasks and understand how these relate to their own tasks and how they are relevant to their goals.
5. Counsellors have the skill necessary to implement their tasks.
6. The tasks of both counsellor and client have sufficient therapeutic potency to facilitate the achievement of the client's goals.

Counsellors, in assuming their role, have responsibility for carrying out another set of tasks which establish and maintain the viability of counselling relationships. These 'professional' tasks are likely to be covered in any code of ethics and practice to which counsellors subscribe and include setting and maintaining professional boundaries, ensuring that a non-exploitative relationship is established and sustained, maintaining confidentiality and making appropriate referrals when the concerns of clients fall outside the counsellors' range of expertise.

While work in the three domains of the alliance is confidential to the counsellor–client pair, it is generally accepted that counsellors need to monitor this work with another professional. Thus, to ensure that both 'professional' and 'change-related' tasks are carried out with skill and integrity, to safeguard the quality of the bond between counsellor and client and to check that counselling has a productive direction, all counsellors are required to undergo regular supervision.

3 W(h)ither non-directive counselling?

When counselling began to become popular in the UK, back in the pioneering days of the 1960s, many people claimed to practise non-directive counselling. At that time it was important for counsellors to distinguish themselves from advice-givers and guidance workers, and this was best done by arguing that they were not offering their clients any direction. To say, at that time, that counsellors were directive was to cast aspersions on the integrity of their work; their principal task was to 'facilitate' their clients by helping them to find their own direction. The counsellor would hold up a mirror before their client, who would emerge from confusion and see in that mirror a way forward.

However, as counselling came of age in the 1970s (and, in particular, the early 1980s), the use of the term 'non-directive' counselling decreased. It is not entirely clear why this happened, but a parallel can be found in the work of Carl Rogers and those who practise in what is now known as the 'person-centred' tradition. In 1942, Rogers published his seminal work *Counseling and Psychotherapy*, in which he made the case for non-directive counselling and in doing so was keen to show how his approach differed from the directive approach of the vocational psychologists of his day on the one hand, and from the medical model approach of contemporary analysts on the other. Non-directive counselling was, at that time, more defined by what the counsellor did *not* do than by what he or she actually *did*. Suffice it to say, non-directive counsellors strove strictly to clarify the client's experience and were criticised if they departed from this restricted brief (see Rogers' comments on the transcript of a therapy case in his 1942 book). Person-centred counselling is very different from its non-directive predecessor, and person-centred counsellors no longer see themselves as non-directive. This is not to say that they give advice or offer guidance, because they do not. However, they realise that it is not possible to be non-directive.

Why am I devoting all this space to a concept that seems to be out of

7

fashion? Because there are still counsellors who describe themselves as
'non-directive': I've met them and, strange to tell, they seem to be
growing in numbers. So here's my attempt to, once and for all, lay the
ghost of non-directiveness.

Let us first consider what, as a non-directive counsellor, you would
actually do in a session. Presumably, to say anything to a client about
her experience involves directing yourself to what you consider she is
saying. Now, given the weight that counsellors place on the importance
of feelings in the lives of people, aren't you going to direct yourself to
the emotional aspects of what your client says? Even if you decide to
say absolutely nothing in a session, isn't that a direction, in the very
same way as indecisiveness involves making a decision to do nothing?
This clearly means (as far as the process of counselling is concerned)
that all counsellors are directive in the sense that they direct themselves to what they consider to be salient aspects of their clients' com-
munications.

But what about when we consider the end product of counselling;
surely counsellors do not direct clients to any given resolution of their
concerns? Surely our raison d'être is to help our clients to decide upon
a direction for themselves? I do not dispute this as long as our clients
do not choose a direction that is likely, in our view, to be defeating for
them or lead to harm others. In other words, counsellors are likely, in
all kinds of elusive ways, to direct clients away from certain paths.

Suppose you are counselling someone and he decides to do voluntary work on behalf of a school for children with cerebral palsy and
wants to give a large donation to the Save the Children Fund. Aren't
you pleased with this outcome? Would you dwell on this and encourage your client to think through all the implications of these decisions?
I doubt it, because you would see the decisions as expressions of your
client's healthy development. But what if the client decides to sell dubious insurance policies to the newly widowed and wants to give a large
donation to the National Front. Would you respond in the same way as
before? Again I doubt it. Nor would counsellors who see themselves as
'non-directive'. Now, it is unlikely that they would come out in the
open and reveal that they are unhappy about the direction the client is
taking: rather, they may dwell subtly on the issue, enquire whether or
not the client has thought through all the issues involved, or (even
more subtly and outside their awareness) may alter their non-verbal
behaviour to indicate their unease. However, by doing so aren't they
still taking a direction, albeit one that is covert? A counsellor can
respect a client's right to choose options that may be self- and other-
defeating even though he or she queries the wisdom of such choices.
Making such queries is directive and I see nothing wrong in that. What
I *do* oppose is counsellors imposing solutions on clients. That kind of
directiveness undermines client autonomy and has no place in the

counselling endeavour.

So let's face it, counsellors are non-directive with respect neither to our interventions nor to the outcome of counselling. Admitting this does not turn us into power-hungry advice givers or 'we know best' do-gooders: it means that we are not neutral in the counselling endeavour. We are involved in that we have values and implicit ideas of healthy client development that influence the direction of our interventions. Once we are aware of this fact we can reflect on the direction we are taking with our clients in order to minimise personal bias and to grapple with the dilemmas of our work. If we are 'non-directive' what is there to grapple with?

To return to Carl Rogers, there is an old joke that ends with the client jumping out of the window and Rogers looking down on the splattered body, saying, 'Splodge' – reflecting to the end. In reality Rogers would have directed himself to prevent the client, forcibly if necessary, from killing himself. To have done otherwise would have been against his values.

So, to paraphrase Sheldon Kopp; if you meet a non-directive counsellor on the road, don't kill him, but do disabuse him.

4 On neglecting the therapeutic relationship

For years now, I've been fending off criticisms of rational–emotive therapy (RET) that its practitioners neglect the therapeutic relationship and are too preoccupied with technique. Critics invariably cite Albert Ellis's interview with Gloria as evidence in their defence. The 'Gloria' videos, for those of you who haven't come across them, show Gloria, a volunteer client with real emotional conflicts, being interviewed by Carl Rogers, Fritz Perls and Albert Ellis. The interviews took place in 1965 and of the four participants only Albert Ellis is alive today.

People who see the Ellis portion are so shocked to see a therapist being overtly active–directive in his approach that they conclude that the relationship is being neglected. This criticism is usually more marked when the Ellis interview is seen directly after the one with Carl Rogers. Rogers is his consistent empathic, respectful and congruent self and whatever criticisms I have heard of his interview with Gloria, neglecting the therapeutic relationship isn't one of them.

Leaving aside the point that Ellis subsequently made (that he was trying to pack too much into the session in an attempt to demonstrate a full range of RET techniques) and also ignoring the fact that the interview was conducted 27 years ago and lasted 18 minutes, is it fair to judge an entire approach to counselling on the basis of one interview, or, indeed, on the basis of one practitioner, albeit the founder of that approach? I hope you will agree that such a judgement, founded on such flimsy evidence, is indeed unfair.

What is needed to determine whether RET therapists neglect the therapeutic relationship? The answer is *research*. I have just read a report of a study that addresses itself to this very issue and want to discuss it here because it helps to put the record straight on RET. The researchers did take the point that Rogers made about assessing the quality of the counselling relationship: that it is necessary to judge such quality from the client's point of view. Furthermore, they used a measure of the therapeutic relationship that taps the core conditions of empathy, warmth and genuineness generally regarded as features of a good quality relationship. Finally, they compared their results with data obtained from previous studies which employed the same questionnaire (the Therapy Relationship Questionnaire, developed by Truax and Carkhuff, well-known researchers respected for their studies on the therapeutic relationship).

A total of 126 clients of 21 RET therapists (including Albert Ellis) completed the questionnaire. The results showed that, in general, RET therapists were rated highly on the core conditions by their clients: indeed, these clients gave their therapists higher ratings on these variables than did clients who, in two earlier studies, consulted non-RET therapists.

This clearly shows that RET therapists, in the main, do not neglect the therapeutic relationship and develop good relationships (as judged by their clients). It also shows that there is no one way to develop good therapeutic relationships and that the active–directive style of RET therapists is no impediment to their development.

One other interesting finding emerged from this study, which perhaps explains why RET therapists have a bad reputation on the therapeutic relationship front. Compared with both experienced and inexperienced RET therapists, Albert Ellis was judged significantly less 'warm' by clients. However, this finding is consistent with Ellis's views on productive counselling relationships: namely that empathy, unconditional acceptance of clients and genuineness are facilitative therapist relationship qualities, but that warmth is not. Ellis does not attempt to convey warmth to his clients and is not experienced by them as very warm. When people see the 'Gloria' interview and other demonstrations conducted by Ellis, I hypothesise that they are struck by his lack of warmth and the active–directive style of his interventions. In doing so, they fail to recognise that, unlike his clients, he is conveying other relationship qualities. Having failed to notice his empathic and genuine stance towards and unconditional acceptance of his clients, observers conclude – wrongly, as this study shows – that he *and* other RET therapists neglect the therapeutic relationship.

This study is certainly not the first to confound the critics. For years, until 1975, opponents of behaviour therapy claimed that its practitioners were preoccupied with technique, to the neglect of relationship variables. This view was reinforced by the behavioural literature in which, up to that time, little emphasis was placed on such variables. In 1975, an important study (conducted by Sloane and colleagues) was published, which compared the effectiveness of psychodynamic therapy with behaviour therapy. One of the virtues of this study was that well-known and respected therapists of both persuasions were employed in the comparison. What surprised many about this study was that both sets of therapists were judged to develop good therapeutic relationships with their clients.

I want to underscore two points here. The first concerns emphasis: while writers on both rational–emotive therapy and behaviour therapy may be guilty of de-emphasising the importance of the quality of therapeutic relationships in the change process – presumably in their quest to convey the distinctive technical elements of each approach – such neglect is not an integral part of either approach. My second point concerns perception. I have argued that Albert Ellis's active–directive style and lack of overt warmth may lead observers to conclude that he is a therapist who neglects the therapeutic relationship. As we have seen, this is directly contradicted by Ellis's clients who, while aware of his style and lack of warmth, still experience him as empathic, accepting and genuine. No doubt some rational–emotive therapists (and behaviour therapists) neglect the importance of developing and maintaining well-bonded, collaborative relationships with their clients, but we now have enough evidence to silence the critics. RET and behaviour therapists, by and large, do *not* neglect the therapeutic relationship; there is more than one way to develop a good quality relationship, and the sooner the 'Gloria' interview with Ellis stops being used as representative of RET the better!

5 To tape or not to tape? The use of audio tapes in counselling and supervision

The use of sound-recording techniques in counselling was pioneered by Carl Rogers and his colleagues in the early days of client-centred therapy. Such recordings enabled Rogers to formulate and test hypotheses concerning the relationship between therapist-offered core conditions and positive client change. The recordings of actual therapy sessions revolutionised research into the counselling process and, it might be argued, prompted the growth of counselling services both in the USA and in the UK. While the use of audio-tape recording of counselling sessions is widespread in the USA, counsellors in the UK are wary of the practice. The aim of this article is to describe my use of audio procedures in my counselling and supervision work and also to deal with some of the issues related to the reluctance of counsellors to implement them in their own practice.

Audio-tape procedures in counselling

I routinely record most of my counselling sessions with clients and I frequently play some of these recordings back at the end of a day's work. Thus I am involved in a process of self-supervision. At the beginning of a counselling relationship I am concerned with checking on my basic interviewing skills with a client on playback. I listen carefully to check whether I am responding to my client from his frame of reference and am alert to those occasions when I appear to have neglected to respond to my client's overt or covert expression of feeling. I also check on whether I have failed to pick up certain cues that my client seems to have given me and find that this helps me to become more aware of such material in subsequent sessions. During this process I endeavour to recapture any thoughts or images I had had in the interview which may have accounted for my failure to respond within my

First published in 1981.

client's frame of reference and my failure to pick up these cues. I find that simply reviewing the session in my mind without recourse to the tape does not provide me with the opportunities to be aware of these issues.

During the middle and later phases of counselling I increasingly employ rational–emotive counselling procedures. At this time, in addition to checking on whether I am succeeding in responding to my client's messages, I endeavour to review my understanding of my client's dynamics from a rational–emotive standpoint. Specific factors that I listen for at this stage are: (1) whether I am exploring inferences which are most relevant to the client's difficulties; (2) whether I am dealing with a sufficiently concrete example of my client difficulties; and (3) whether I have helped the client to identify all the feelings related to these inferences and situations. Through listening to the tape of the session I sometimes discover that progress is being held up because I am exploring less relevant situations, feelings and inferences.

My opinion is that between-session assignments are helpful in facilitating client change. While listening to the playback I am concerned to check whether the assignment has been negotiated and agreed upon by both parties – in my experience between-session assignments are most helpful when such mutuality is achieved.

Rational–emotive therapy is an educational therapy and its effectiveness depends on the extent to which clients understand the concepts which I as a rational–emotive counsellor introduce. To help clients in such a learning process I often suggest that they take a taped copy of the session home to review several times between sessions. In my experience, clients report that this appreciably aids the counselling process. My clients have reported that listening to the tapes between sessions helps them to become clearer both about their own problems and about issues that we have discussed in the session. I invariably check with a client at the beginning of the subsequent session their reactions to listening to the tape. When certain clients report that they have been discouraged by the listening process I may cease such a procedure but deal with the issues which surround their discouragement in the session. Thus, I would advocate that suggesting that clients listen to tapes of their counselling sessions should be employed flexibly.

When I suggest to a client that we record our sessions I am honest about the purposes of so doing. I state that listening to the recordings of the sessions helps me to help them more effectively. I state that I am supervised in my counselling work and that my supervisor may from time to time hear recordings of our sessions, but that no other person will. I also stress to the client that if he is apprehensive about our sessions being recorded then I will not record them, and I am particularly on the lookout for non-verbal cues which may indicate reluctance and strive to bring these out into the open. What I am endeavouring to obtain from my client is their *informed consent* to the procedures that I am suggesting. I find that if I am honest and present the issue about recordings in a way which also gives my client the opportunity to state his or her reactions, then I find that the great majority of clients are willing for our sessions to be recorded. Those few clients who do not agree to our sessions being recorded have not in my experience been adversely affected by my raising the issue. When I suggest that clients take tapes home with them to listen to between sessions I enquire whether they intend to play the tape to a third party. Informed consent is applicable to both counsellor and client.

After I have listened to a tape of a counselling session I wipe the tape clean. If I have reason to keep a particular session then I ensure that the recording is locked away. I also suggest that my clients keep tapes in a safe place, particularly if they are concerned that the tape should not be heard by a third party. The issue of security concerning the retention of tapes needs to be thought through very carefully by counsellors intending to record their sessions. Such an issue is particularly relevant to me because I am supervised by a colleague in America. I send her tapes of my sessions by air mail and am careful to package them in a secure manner with all identifying marks removed. I would recommend that counsellors who wish to have their tapes supervised by mail should send their tapes by recorded delivery.

The use of audio tapes in supervision

When I supervise the work of other counsellors I use many of the procedures that I employ in my self-supervision. Thus, I endeavour to listen to the ability of the supervisee to respond to the client from the client's frame of reference. I offer feedback on ways in which they could improve their empathic responding. It is extremely difficult to do this without listening to actual counselling interchanges. I am often able to detect patterns of unhelpful responding in my supervisees through listening to tapes (which I would be unable to do without having recourse to taped sessions). For example, some supervisees have a tendency to ask closed rather than open questions with clients, even though they may be able to ask open-ended questions in role-play situations which may be enacted in a supervisory session. Other patterns of unhelpful responding that often emerge from the tapes are focusing on content to the exclusion of responding to feelings, focusing on responding to feelings to the exclusion of content and avoidance of responding to certain affect-laden areas.

Another advantage for me as a supervisor in listening to tapes is that I am able to get a better picture of clients if I hear them express themselves. Sometimes I get a very different picture of clients when I actually hear them expressing themselves than when I hear supervisees talking about clients. Focusing on the discrepancy in supervision is really only possible if one has an opportunity to hear the client.

I often employ Norman Kagan's 'Interpersonal Process Recall' methods in conjunction with taped material. Supervisees are often able to identify the thoughts and images that they experience in the session through listening to the tapes, something they are often unable to report spontaneously in more standard supervisory settings. For example, I was recently supervising a tape when I noticed that the counsellor's voice suddenly dropped. I replayed the portion of the tape to the counsellor and suggested that she listen and try to identify any thoughts and images that she might have been having at that particular time. In listening to the tape again the counsellor identified that at that point in the interview she briefly felt overwhelmed with guilt concerning her own mother (the client was talking about her mother). Listening to the tape again provided this supervisee with an opportunity to identify a fleeting but relevant feeling which *may* not have been identified through standard supervision procedures.

When counsellors begin recording their sessions for supervision, they report that they feel self-conscious. They report that having the tape recorder present interferes with their ability to listen attentively to clients. In my experience this is a short-lived phase and, provided that the counsellor persists with recording sessions, the self-consciousness soon fades. Some counsellors are, however, overwhelmed with feelings of anxiety concerning the presence of the tape recorder, to the extent that they are immobilised. Such counsellors are recommended not to persist with recording such sessions, although they may be encouraged to explore the meaning of their overwhelming anxiety and perhaps return to recording when this has been successfully worked through.

Some issues concerning the use of audio tapes in counselling

Counsellors are often against audio-taping sessions for a number of reasons. First, they claim that this is a breach of confidentiality. It is my view that this is an incorrect notion, if one considers the concept of professional confidentiality. For me, professional confidentiality encompasses presenting a case or playing a tape for supervision. Counsellors who are against the use of tapes because it breaches confidentiality normally have no qualms about talking about their clients in supervision, possibly also constituting a breach of confidentiality. My argument is that counsellors who employ tapes should be honest and ask for the client's permission to play tapes to their supervisors. I wonder how many counsellors who do not use tapes ask for their clients' permission to present their cases at a case discussion meeting?

The second issue that counsellors raise concerning the use of tapes is that it may harm the client. In my experience there is very little evidence for this. As I mentioned before, the vast majority of my clients can understand the reason for taping and readily agree to it. Those few who are apprehensive show no signs of being damaged by my raising the issue with them. My hunch on this matter is that concern about potential damage to clients is really a manifestation of the counsellor's projected anxiety. For example, when I suggest that two of my supervisees role-play a situation where the counsellor is introducing the notion of recording sessions with a client, invariably the supervisee plays a suspicious and reluctant client. This occurs with such frequency and is in such contrast to actual experience that I feel that my hunch has a great deal of validity. Indeed, in my experience counsellors are far more anxious about recording sessions (albeit initially) than clients are.

The third and final issue that I wish to deal with concerning counsellors' objections to the use of taping concerns their fear that once it has become known that they are recording their counselling sessions prospective clients will be frightened off. This I believe to be a more realistic anxiety, although such a notion may be difficult to investigate, as it is difficult to ascertain whether prospective clients have been dissuaded from approaching a counsellor because they have learnt that the counsellor in question uses tape recorders in his work. This area deserves further study to determine whether such an anxiety is realistic or perhaps another manifestation of projected anxiety. One way to test such a notion is to look at the attendance records of counselling services which have recently instituted the use of tape recorders into their everyday practice and to determine whether that service experienced a decline in new clients. If any counsellors have any evidence concerning this issue then I would be glad to receive it.

Part II

Flexibility in counselling

6 If at first you don't succeed, stop fluttering your wings

On a recent holiday, I had an experience which at the time seemed commonplace, albeit poignant. However, the more I thought about it, the more it seemed that the experience had something to teach me about the practice of counselling.

One evening after dinner my wife and I took coffee in a small alcove in the hotel where we were staying. While we were relaxing, a large moth flew into the alcove and tried to fly out of the main window, which was fixed shut. Seeing the plight of the moth, I opened a side window, hoping that it might notice this escape route and make good its getaway. However, the moth, blind to my attempt to be helpful, continued to flutter its wings in the hope that it would eventually fly through the large, closed window. Realising that a more interventive approach was called for, I got up and tried to guide the moth gently towards the smaller open window with the palm of my hand. The moth responded to my manoeuvre by lowering itself and increasing the rate of its fluttering. The more I persisted with my gentle approach, the more the moth lowered itself and the faster it fluttered its wings. At this point it seemed to me that a more drastic approach was called for. Thus, I increased the force of my guiding hand movement and with three flicks I succeeded in helping the moth make its escape.

There seem to be four lessons that can be learned from this. First, some people, faced with a problem, approach it in a stereotypical manner. It is as if they have only one 'solution' in their repertoire and they are going to use this by hook or by crook. Faced with failure, these people redouble their efforts and pour more energy into the unsuccessful 'solution'. They are just like the moth who tried to fly through the closed window and increased its fluttering when its initial attempt to solve the problem failed.

Secondly, some clients are very reluctant to give up coping strategies that don't work. Faced with our gentle counselling interventions where we may point out better ways of solving their problems, they respond by redoubling their efforts to make their unsuccessful 'solution' work, even though they show some evidence of having heard what we have said. The moth did respond to my gentle approach by lowering itself away from my hand, but in doing so it increased its effort to fly through the fixed window by trying to fly forward ever faster.

Thirdly, we may be able to help such clients to solve their immediate problems by increasing the force of our interventions, but what will they have learned in the process? What will the moth do the next time it encounters a fixed window? It will approach the problem in the same way as before I intervened: in short, it will have learned nothing.

I am very much in agreement with my old friend and erstwhile colleague, Richard Nelson-Jones, who argues that one of the goals of counselling is to teach clients a broad repertoire of life skills that they can use flexibly when faced with life stressors. However, occasionally we will meet clients who are not open to such an approach. In such situations, we will be faced with the choice of bringing about a solution to a client's immediate problem by using a forceful (and perhaps even a dramatic) intervention or of doing what we normally do without effecting any change.

This brings me to my fourth and final point. Sometimes in counselling we need to do what we normally *don't* do to help the client out of a seemingly impossible jam. I normally don't go around forcefully flicking moths through open windows, but am glad I did so on this occasion. My fantasy is that had I not done so the moth would still be there, fluttering its ever-tiring little wings and searching in vain for the escape that would never come.

We can only implement interventions that, for us, are out of the ordinary if we are prepared to be flexible. If we are prepared to practice only according to the guidelines of our preferred orientations, we may not be acting in the interests of some of our clients. In such cases we, too, may find ourselves fluttering our therapeutic wings against the closed minds of our clients. Of course, abandoning our usual ways of working means that we will have to face levels of discomfort that we would normally strive to avoid – which brings me to the subject of my next piece.

7 The discomfort of being a counsellor

I recently sat on a committee which was considering a Diploma course in counselling. One of the aims of the course was to enable trainees to choose a way of working with which they were comfortable. Now, at first sight this seems quite reasonable. After all we don't want counsellors to be uncomfortable in their way of working, do we? Well, yes, frankly I do. I'm not against counsellors choosing their theoretical orientations as long as they realise that all these frameworks have distinct limitations and that if we, as counsellors, are going to be of help to a wide variety of clients this means, in all probability, that we need to become proficient in a wide variety of counselling interventions. And, here is the rub, we may well feel uncomfortable in using some of these interventions, but are we going to allow our personal comfort to stand in the way of our professional development?

Now, in order for counsellors to know which interventions are effective for which clients at which points in the counselling process, we are going to have to acquaint ourselves with the work of both practitioners from other orientations and counselling researchers. This implies that we need to read widely and consult research journals which, in turn, means that we are going to have to make ourselves uncomfortable in grappling with unfamiliar language and concepts on the one hand, and the complexities of research design and methodology on the other.

There is some truth in the oft-quoted point that different approaches to counselling and therapy are equivalent in therapeutic effectiveness. However, there is also evidence that for some specific problems specific therapeutic interventions are called for. For example, if you are counselling someone who has, among other concerns, a compulsion to wash his or her hands, unless you use some form of response prevention, therapeutic progress on this problem is likely to be limited, no matter how warm, empathic and genuine you are. Now these qualities may

First published in 1992.

encourage your client to take part in a response prevention programme, but they will not on their own help him or her to overcome
encrusted obsessive–compulsive habits. 'Well,' I hear you say, 'I would
refer the person for specialised help on such concerns.' Yes, you could,
but think of the implications of this. Instead of making yourself temporarily uncomfortable and learning a range of interventions that are
seemingly incompatible with your preferred therapeutic approach, you
remain comfortable, but limited as a complete practitioner

The worst excesses of counsellor comfort occur when we consider
the staffing of some counselling agencies. I once saw an advert for a
gestalt counsellor to join a counselling service that was staffed by two
other gestaltists. This is ludicrous, but before gestalt therapists become
enraged, I would consider it ludicrous for a counselling agency to be
staffed by counsellors from any single orientation. It is ludicrous simply
because it is not in the interests of clients; rather it is in the interests of
counsellors who wish to be comfortable with one another.

If we really wish to honour the uniqueness of our clients, we need
to accept the simple fact that different clients need different counselling interventions. This means two things: first, as individual counsellors we need to broaden our counselling repertoire; secondly, we
need to staff our counselling services with counsellors from a broad
range of orientations who are interested in learning from each other
and in so doing will broaden their practice.

Doing both of these things will, of course, mean that we will have to
put up with the discomfort that these challenges will bring. However,
tolerating and even welcoming such discomfort will be in the best
interests of us as counsellors, the profession of counselling and, most
importantly, the mental health and development of clients.

8 The counselling field needs shadchonim . . .

When people decide to seek counselling, it is usually after a period of grappling with their concerns on their own or after seeking help from a variety of informal helpers. Thus, they may have tried to share their concerns with family or friends; they may have consulted their GP, talked things over with a member of the clergy or written to an agony aunt or uncle. They may even have read one of the plethora of self-help books that line the shelves of book shops. It is when these attempts at getting help fail that professional assistance is considered seriously. Although increasing numbers of people are seeking counselling, it is usually not a step that is considered without one or more of the above measures having been tried first.

When the decision to see a counsellor is made, the first hurdle presents itself: how does one find a counsellor? There are obvious steps that the potential client can take. She can ask one of the informal helpers in whom she previously confided if they know of someone; she can ask around to discover if anyone she knows has seen a counsellor who has been helpful; she can contact a professional association and ask for a list of local practitioners. She can even consult *Yellow Pages*. All of these steps, however, are fraught with problems.

For example, the personal recommendation from a friend who has found a particular counsellor helpful is seductive. However, it does not follow that our potential client will find a counsellor helpful just because his friend was helped by that counsellor. He may have very different concerns from his friend, have very different ideas about how he can be best helped, or the interpersonal match between our client and the counsellor may be less conducive to a productive working alliance than the match between the counsellor and the friend.

Consulting a professional organisation also has its difficulties. If the organisation is a broad, national one, then probably the best it can offer is a list of accredited counsellors in the client's geographical area. While this serves as some protection to our client, she still has to do a lot of shopping around if she is going to find a counsellor who is 'right' for her. Assuming that she consults an organisation which is very closely associated with a particular approach to counselling, then if she is offered an assessment interview, the chances are that she will eventually be referred to a practitioner who practises that approach. Now, that is fine if the client has sought out the organisation because she wants, for example, a psychodynamic counsellor and her concerns can be productively addressed by a practitioner of that approach. However, if such is not the case, then the client will have to take pot luck.

Taking pot luck is certainly the case if our client consults *Yellow Pages*. Counsellors who advertise there may (or may not) be *bona fide*. What unites them is their decision to spend quite a lot of money advertising their services. As far as I know there is no relationship between counsellor competence and willingness to advertise therapeutic services. Many professional organisations frown on counsellors advertising in this way and therefore counsellors who do so may, and I repeat *may*, be more suspect than counsellors who do not so advertise. Thus, clients who choose this method of finding a counsellor need to heed the refrain 'caveat emptor'.

Is there a better alternative to these rather haphazard undertakings? I believe that there is, but, as far as I know, it is infrequently practised. This alternative involves the field of counselling making use of therapeutic shadchonim. A shadchen, in traditional Eastern European Jewish circles, was a maker of marital matches (known as shidukhs). He or she would arrange introductions for single Jewish men and women who wished to get married. Now, in order for shadchonim to do their job well, they needed a thorough knowledge of their potential clientèle (i.e. the body of unmarried people in the local community). They needed to know the likes and dislikes of these young people, their strengths and weaknesses, their personality and interactive styles, their aspirations and attitudes, and their views of married life. In short, shadchonim needed to have a plethora of information to enable them to suggest potentially fruitful shidukhs. Their knowledge was bought and paid for to help everyone concerned save precious time. They could not, of course, guarantee that their selections would yield productive relationships, but their reputation hinged upon success. Poor shadchonim quickly went out of business.

What I would like to see in the counselling field is therapeutic shadchonim. But how would they operate? – in a very similar way to the shadchonim of old. They would first gain a detailed knowledge of the counsellors in their geographical location. Thus, they would need to discover a practitioner's orientation, specialisms, personality and interactive style, strengths and weaknesses as well as her fee structure and general working pattern. Then they would interview potential clients. They would not only need to know the clients' presenting concerns, but also should gather information on, among other things, the clients' views on the length of counselling, who might be the best person to help them and why, whether they would respond better to an exploratory style of counselling or one that is more structured, and what they can afford. Therapeutic shadchonim would need to be sensitive to the fact that certain clients' preferences for counselling may be anti-therapeutic, but in general they would seek to effect productive counselling shidukhs, based on all the information at their disposal. Like their religious counterparts, their reputation would be based on the success of their matches, and effective shadchonim could be studied to discover the secrets of their success.

It is likely, at least at first, that therapeutic shadchonim would themselves be counsellors. This would mean, of course, that they could not refer to themselves. After all, religious shadchonim did not seek to marry the young people who sought their services.

Now, if this idea takes off, the astute and enterprising will be able to see the possibilities inherent in this new development. We could have diploma courses for aspiring shadchonim, supervisors of practising shadchonim and training courses for these supervisors, schemes for the accreditation of shadchonim, etc. But, of course, this is a whole other issue!

9 ... And bespoke tailors too

If the counselling field needs shadchonim, it also needs the therapeutic equivalent of another traditional Jewish figure: the bespoke tailor. Bespoke tailors are a dying breed, but in their heyday they made their reputation by ensuring that they provided their customers with suits that fitted exactly. Such tailors practised 'made-to-measure' tailoring as a fine art. From the very first contact to the time when the customer left his shop with the finished garment, the bespoke tailor devoted himself to the task of ensuring that the customer got the right suit for the right occasion and one that fitted him 'like a glove'. Not that the bespoke tailor was guided by his customer's every whim. Rather, he established what his customer wanted the suit for and, if the customer's choice did not meet his own requirements, the tailor found a way to bring this to the customer's attention. The bespoke tailor never tried to hoodwink one of his customers for short-term profit. Like the shadchen, the bespoke tailor made his living by establishing and maintaining a reputation for high quality. His aim was to keep a customer for life and to acquire new customers by recommendation. Bad bespoke tailors, like bad shadchonim, soon went out of business.

To acquire this reputation, a bespoke tailor had to master a wide range of tailoring styles and skills as well as a flexible interpersonal style for dealing with his many different customers. He would not have survived long in business if he could only make wedding suits in a certain style for a certain type of customer. He was definitely not trained in a tailoring school with unfavourable staff–student ratios! Rather, he undertook a lengthy apprenticeship with a master bespoke tailor. Over the years he passed on his many skills to his own apprentices and in this way the craft was kept alive.

What, then, is the therapeutic equivalent of the bespoke tailor? A bespoke counsellor would be someone who first and foremost would be able to relate well with a broad range of clients. She would be able to vary her interpersonal style both between cases and within a given case. She would be what that doyen of bespoke therapists, Arnold Lazarus, calls an authentic chameleon. Thus, she would be able to move adroitly from an empathic, exploratory style to an active–directive teaching style when it was called for. She would know when to self-disclose and when not; she would be able to be informal in her therapeutic delivery with some clients and distant and businesslike with others. Above all, she would know her interpersonal limits and, without self-reproach, would refer some clients to colleagues who would be better matched, interpersonally, to help them.

Conceptually, the bespoke counsellor would have a broad perspective on psychological problems – how they arise, factors involved in their perpetuation and how therapeutic change may be facilitated. He may well have his conceptual predilections, but would be able to look beyond these when necessary. He would keep in mind that humans are thinking, feeling, sensing, acting, imagining, interpersonally oriented and, some would say, spiritual organisms whose psychological mechanisms interact crucially with both environmental and biological factors. He would, thus, have what Lazarus calls a multimodal perspective on his work rather than a unimodal, bimodal or even trimodal perspective. Consequently, he would read widely in the literature and would be a member of a diverse number of professional associations.

Technically, the bespoke counsellor would be proficient in a number of areas. She would be able to translate her empathy for and respect of her clients into ways of communicating that would take her clients deeper into their explorations of themselves. She would speak with economy, clarity and with full regard for the comprehension levels of her clients. She would neither patronise nor obfuscate and her use of jargon would be minimal. She would be knowledgeable of and skilful in the use of so-called therapeutic techniques. Her knowledge of the research literature would guide her in the selection of such techniques which she would explain and tailor to the unique circumstances of her clients.

In all this, the bespoke counsellor would clearly acknowledge that counselling techniques are best employed in the context of a well-bonded, goal-directed therapeutic alliance. However, he would also acknowledge that, under certain conditions, the therapeutic relationship is insufficient for the promotion of therapeutic change and that withholding the use of tried and tested techniques would constitute bad practice. Being a bespoke counsellor, he would frequently tailor his interventions to suit the requirements of his clients. However, once again, his knowledge of the research would lead him to work in a non-bespoke, 'off the peg' way with clients experiencing certain problems. Thus, he would utilise the research that showed that a standardised intervention is more effective than a tailor-made intervention in the treatment of simple phobias. The best bespoke tailors realised that, for certain occasions, an 'off the peg' uniform was the order of the day. While the bespoke counsellor would be guided by research evidence with respect to technique selection, he would know that we are far from having a comprehensive menu of techniques for specific problems. Thus, if necessary, he would be prepared to use techniques that have not been validated by research. However, he would be wary of the ephemeral nature of many novel techniques. He would know only too well that the fad of today may well be consigned to the realm of quackery tomorrow.

With respect to working in what I call the 'therapeutic arenas', the bespoke counsellor would ideally be able to work skilfully in individual, couple, family and group counselling, although practically she may have deficits here. For example, unless she has had experience in working with children, she may not have the skills to work in family counselling when there are young children present: in which eventuality, she would probably refer such cases to family-oriented practitioners. She would be able to move flexibly from arena to arena within a given case, when necessary, but would be fully cognisant of the complexities and problems of doing so. Here, as throughout, she would discuss such issues in peer supervision with other like-minded experienced bespoke counsellors.

I could go on, but I think I have made my point. Such therapeutic *ubermenschen* are very thin on the ground. Writing as I do in the UK in 1992, I see little hope that our training activities are geared up to produce them. We rarely use the apprenticeship approach to training and, even if we did, where are the master bespoke counsellors to serve as expert role models? The one light in the darkness is the emerging development of integrative and eclectic approaches to counselling. This movement may widen the horizons of our still predominantly unimodal field and produce, in the twenty-first century, practitioners capable of serving as models for the bespoke counsellors of the future. In the meantime, we need to rely on therapeutic shadchonim to hold the fort and ensure that, if clients are not going to get bespoke counselling, they will at least get 'off the peg' help that will, more or less, fit.

Part III

The semantics of counselling

10 Counselling, semantic precision and pedantry

My counselling trainees often consider me a pedant when it comes to their use of words. I frequently ask them what they mean when they employ certain terms, and when they reply I often have to encourage them to clarify their responses. Am I the pedant they think I am or is there a method in my seeming madness? Well, first, let me hold my hand up and admit to being somewhat obsessive–compulsive. As I write this I can hear peals of laughter from my students at the word 'somewhat'. Some of them no doubt think that the 'D' in OCD (obsessive–compulsive disorder) stands for Dryden. This notwithstanding, I do favour precision and clarity, and certainly do not like the vague and the imprecise. So, yes, these enquiries concerning the meaning of words certainly stem, in part, from characterological factors.

However, there is another reason why I question my students closely on the meaning of their words: one which transcends my personality. I do so because I firmly believe that effective counselling is, in part, predicated on the clarity of communication between counsellor and client. It is crucial that both understand what the other is communicating and, in my experience, what often impedes the accuracy of such understanding is the vague, imprecise use of language. So when I ask trainees to clarify what they mean – no doubt in my idiosyncratic 'OC' manner – I am urging them to be more effective communicators, both inside the counselling session and in training and supervision settings.

Over the years, my trainees have developed lists of words to which I particularly object. While the words on these lists change from year to year depending upon whatever lexical bee I have in my semantic bonnet, there are some hardy perennials and, in the remainder of this piece, I will devote myself to these.

Expectation

A review of the research on clients' expectations of counselling and therapy which appeared in 1979 made the telling point that research workers in this area had not distinguished between two types of expectations (anticipations and preferences), thus making it difficult for people to make valid conclusions from this literature. Thus, if a client was asked about her expectations of counselling, her reply could be taken as what she thought would happen or what she hoped (or preferred) would happen. These, of course, could be very different. Our client might, for example, anticipate being offered a brief contract with a distant male 'clinician' who would give advice, while at the same time preferring a longer term, open-ended contract with a warm, empathic female counsellor. Clearly the term 'expectation' cannot cover both situations without further clarification. Now, let us add to this confusing state of affairs another meaning of 'expectation'. More than a few clients stay in counselling that has failed to live up to their own expectations. While occasionally they mean that they have fallen short of what they anticipated achieving or hoped they would achieve, more frequently they seem to mean that they have failed to meet their self-imposed demands. Here, the term has a rigid, absolutist connotation. So 'expectations' can mean anticipations, preferences, hopes and even demands. When counsellor and client or trainer and trainee use the word without clarification, there is a reasonably good chance that they will misunderstand each other with unfortunate consequences for the subsequent process of counselling or training.

Appropriate

My next grouse concerns the word 'appropriate', but for a different reason – when used by counsellors, novice and experienced alike, it rarely communicates anything. The term is often used in supervision by counsellors when discussing reasons for their interventions (e.g. 'I did it because it felt (or seemed) appropriate at the time'). Now, I am not against intuition in counselling, nor am I an opponent of counsellor spontaneity. However, I *do* expect (meaning hope!) that counsellors can give cogent reasons for their intuitive and spontaneous interventions. To say: 'I did that because it was appropriate', or 'I said that because it felt right' tells us nothing. Being able to account for one's responses to clients in a cogent fashion, without resorting to post hoc justifications, involves disciplined introspection. Relying on the criterion of appropriateness without further elaboration reveals a sloppy, undisciplined approach to our craft and, in my opinion, this just will not do.

Around

I've almost finished letting off steam, but before I close, and at the risk of getting myself really hot under my linguistic collar, let me address myself to the seemingly innocuous word 'around' – as in the statement often heard from counsellors: 'The client spoke around the issue of dependency [or anger or whatever].' Now, what is wrong with the use of 'around' here? My problem is that it is far too tentative and vague: if the client has been talking about dependency (or anger or whatever), why not use a more precise term such as 'about' or 'on'. If the client has been more vague in her exploration, why not make this clear in the description? Counsellors often use the word 'around' to describe both precise and imprecise phenomena, so when it is employed, one does not know what is being communicated. My hunch is that when the word 'around' is used in such contexts, one of two things is happening: first, the word may be employed to help the counsellor 'get by' (the sub-text is often: 'I am helping the client to explore his concerns, but don't question me too closely on what I am doing'); secondly, the word may be a sign that the counsellor is engaging in sloppy thinking. So, watch out for the word 'around' – its use repays exploration.

In closing, I realise that I have made myself vulnerable to all kinds of wisecracks. For example, it won't be too long before someone comes up to me and says: 'Windy, I want to discuss something with you. It's around the issue of the appropriateness of expectations!' If this happens, I will take it in good heart and will draw comfort from the knowledge that I have got my message across.

11 Put-downs, insults and other disparaging remarks

Language is a very powerful tool. It can transform what some consider to be good practice into what others see as bad practice; thus, what may be viewed as 'caring' by some may be seen as 'indulgent' by others. Language can take the sting out of negative acts; thus lying and uttering falsehoods can be explained away as being 'economical with the truth'. And words can help remove the stigma from various 'conditions'; thus, my wife jokes that she is not 'short', but 'vertically challenged'. I, of course, am not 'balding'. No, indeed, I have 'a high forehead'. The fact that it begins at the back of my head is neither here nor there. Joking aside, the words that we employ are so potent that they can start feuds or heal rifts, soothe emotional pain or deepen anguish, facilitate understanding or promote ill-will.

One would hope that in the field of counselling and psychotherapy, the words that we use to describe the views and practices of fellow professionals with whom we disagree might demonstrate a respectful, albeit demurring, attitude, based on a willingness to understand a different perspective. If so, one would hope in vain. For our field is rife with put-downs, insults and other disparaging remarks made of those with whom we disagree. Thankfully, most of these remarks are made verbally and out of earshot of the other, although occasionally they do appear in print.

Why do we do this? My view is that we do it for two main reasons. First, we use put-downs, insults and the like to feel superior. If other counsellors practise a form of therapy that, for example, 'indulges' clients, then this reflects favourably on the 'non-indulgent' work that we do. Secondly, they help to confirm us in the rightness of our views. If those therapists are 'superficial' because they do not work with the transference, say, then why on earth should we spend much time trying to understand the nature of their work, since they are so obviously wrong? Such language serves to protect us in the cocoon-like illusion of our superiority and preserves us from grappling productively with cognitive dissonance. An apocryphal story about a trainee analyst has it that he said: 'The wonderful thing about psychoanalysis is that even if the patient does not improve, you're comforted in the knowledge that, at least, you've been doing the right thing.' Now, of course, this could easily have been said by a practitioner of any other orientation. The point is that if one truly believes that one can never be troubled by disconfirming data, then one will not experience the discomfort of such dissonance. Putting down the work of others serves the same purpose – it wards off the threat of having our cherished views challenged.

Let us consider some of the put-downs, insults etc., that one can, without making too much effort, hear expressed in our field. Let us start with person-centred counselling. Person-centred counsellors are seen as 'naïve', 'wishy-washy', 'goody-goodies' who 'just repeat back the last thing their clients say to them'. They are said to practise a 'rambling', 'aimless', 'unfocused' type of counselling and are said to have an 'overly positive, Pollyanna-ish view of human nature'. While most counsellors from other traditions recognise that the core conditions of empathy, respect and congruence are, in fact, facilitative, this is seen as being all right 'as far as it goes' which presumably is not very far! 'Everybody in the field does that, don't they?' and 'it's OK as a prelude to the real work' – which again means whatever approach the critic practises – are other views commonly expressed about this approach to counselling.

Psychoanalytic counsellors are seen to be 'preoccupied' or 'fixated' with the past. One psychiatrist, it is said, used to refer to this form of therapy as 'a bit of how's your father'! Many critics focus on the 'quasireligious' nature of the approach and experimentally minded psychologists delight in focusing on the 'untestability' of its theories and the 'lack of scientific evidence demonstrating its efficacy' as a therapeutic approach. One eminent psychologist defines psychoanalysis as 'a means of taking money away from people on the pretext that one is doing good'! Another eminent figure, this time in the field of psychotherapy, is less polite. His view is that psychoanalytic therapy is 'horseshit'.

Behavioural and cognitive–behavioural counsellors are particular targets for barbed comments. Behavioural therapists are seen as 'mechanistic', 'manipulative' and 'superficial' therapists who 'neglect' the counsellor–client relationship and who 'insist that the private events of our thoughts and feelings are of no importance, just froth and bubble'. Cognitive–behavioural counsellors 'tell' clients what to think, teach clients to 'think positively' and, like their behavioural colleagues, 'ignore' clients' feelings. Rational–emotive counsellors are especially singled out for choice insults. They are seen as 'argumentative' people who engage in 'benign bullying'. Based on stereotypes of the founder of RET, Albert Ellis, they are seen as 'foul-mouthed', 'cold' practitioners who 'bombard' their clients with an endless stream of words.

Counsellors who advocate an eclectic approach to their work do not escape such invective. They are seen as 'muddle-headed' folk who have 'both feet planted firmly in the air'. They are deemed to subscribe to a 'mish-mash of theories, a hugger-mugger of procedures, a gallimaufry of therapies and a charivaria of activities'.

How can we legitimately encourage our clients to respect the different views expressed by other people in their lives, when we find it so difficult to tolerate, let alone respect, the different views of our colleagues? Maybe we need to heal ourselves first! In doing so, we have to tackle our need to be superior and be prepared, as I have said earlier in this book, to tolerate discomfort, especially the discomfort that comes from cognitive dissonance. If we do neither of these things, then the put-downs, the insults and the other disparaging remarks will continue to the detriment of both ourselves and our clients.

12 The semantics of rationality

One of the most profound influences on my approach to counselling has been the work of Albert Ellis, the founder of rational–emotive therapy (see p. 3). However, whenever I lecture on this therapeutic system, people get hung up on the words 'rational' and 'irrational'. They give these terms all kinds of connotations that are inaccurate when one considers the meaning of the words as they are used in RET. So, in this piece I shall consider some of the objections people have to these words. But first, what do these words mean in RET theory? Because they are most frequently employed in RET as adjectives to discriminate a person's rational beliefs from his or her irrational beliefs, I will consider the words within this context.

Actually, the words 'irrational' and 'rational' have four interrelated meanings in RET theory. In describing these meanings, I will consider the word 'irrational' first.

The primary meaning of the word 'irrational' in RET is *dogmatic, rigid* or *absolutist*. Thus, irrational beliefs take the form of musts, absolute shoulds, have to's, etc. Rational beliefs, in contrast, are those which are non-dogmatic, flexible and preferential in nature. They frequently take the form of wishes, wants, desires, etc.

The second meaning of the word 'irrational' is *illogical*. A specific irrational belief (e.g. 'I must do well in my exams') follows neither logically from the person's specific rational belief ('I want to do well in my exams, but there's no reason why I must excel in them'), nor from the person's general rational belief ('Generally, I prefer to do well in my activities, but I don't have to excel in them'), whereas the person's specific rational belief does logically follow from his (in this case) general rational belief.

The third meaning of the term 'irrational' is *that which is inconsistent with reality*. If there was a law of the universe which stated that the person mentioned above must do well in his exams, then there would be no way he could fail to obey such a law. Obviously, it is within the bounds of possibility for him not to do well in the exams, therefore the belief 'I must do well in my exams' is inconsistent with reality. On the other hand, both the specific and general rational beliefs mentioned above are consistent with the reality of the person's desires and acknowledge that such desires do not have to be fulfilled.

The final meaning of the word 'irrational' is *that which interferes with a person's healthy adjustment* (both intrapersonal and interpersonal), *his happiness and the pursuit of his personally meaningful goals and purposes*. If we take the belief 'I must do well in my exams', you will see that this will lead the person (1) to experience anxiety before taking his exams, an emotion which will probably interfere with his task-focused concentration; and (2) to become depressed after the exams should he not do well, an emotion which will impede his healthy adjustment to this negative event. On the other hand, 'rational' means that which promotes healthy adjustment and happiness, and aids the pursuit of personally meaningful goals and purposes. Thus, the rational belief 'I want to do well in my exams, but there's no reason why I have to excel in them' will ensure that he will be concerned (but not anxious) about the prospect of not doing well. These feelings of concern will encourage the person to focus on the task of studying for the exams rather than on a plethora of non-task-related thoughts (as would happen if the person was anxious). If it transpired that the person did not do well in his exams, his rational belief would lead him to feel sad (but not depressed) – an emotion which would encourage him to mourn and move on to adjust constructively to this negative event.

In summary, rational beliefs in RET theory are beliefs that are: (1) non-absolutist and flexible; (2) logical; (3) consistent with reality; and (4) tend to enhance healthy adjustment, happiness and the pursuit of important goals. Irrational beliefs, by contrast, are beliefs that are: (1) absolutist; (2) illogically derived from the person's preferences; (3) inconsistent with reality; and (4) tend to interfere with adjustment, happiness and goal-directed action.

People who either do not know these four meanings of rationality/irrationality or choose to ignore them bring their own connotations to these words and as a result seriously misrepresent RET theory. The first misrepresentation of the word 'rational' is that it means unemotional. As shown above, this is clearly untrue. The person who believed rationally 'I want to well in my exams, but I do not have to excel in them' was shown to experience concern before the exams and sadness if he did not do well. This is a far cry from the Mr Spock-like response of unfeeling logic that is implicit in the 'unemotional' criticism.

The second misrepresentation of the term 'rational' is related to the first. It is that rationality encourages indifference. Again this is false. As I have shown, rational beliefs are, inter alia, preferential in nature. Thus, when people are thinking rationally they are thinking on the basis of their desires. Indifference implies the absence of desires: someone who is indifferent does not care whether he does well in his exams or not.

The third misrepresentation of the word 'rational' is that it means that you apply cold reason to human emotional problems. While reason *is* applied to such problems in RET in that clients are encouraged to use the four criteria of rationality (discussed above) in challenging their irrational beliefs, this process is hardly cold. As I have already shown, rationality does not preclude emotion and RET therapists employ a host of emotive and humorous techniques in the service of applied rationality. It is when people passionately challenge their irrational beliefs that they begin to effect change – challenging such beliefs in a cool, dispassionate way is rarely sufficient in this respect.

The fourth misrepresentation of 'rational' is that it promotes thought to the exclusion of action in dealing with emotional and behavioural problems. This is untrue because RET theory states that personal change comes about when people act on their rational beliefs, rather than when they just think rationally in the comfort of their armchairs.

Misrepresentations of the word 'irrational' tend to fall into two main categories. First, some people think that beliefs that are irrational are crazy, insane, demented or psychotic. While irrational beliefs are self-defeating in that they lead to disturbed emotions and unproductive forms of behaviour, they are not psychotic in nature. For this reason some RET therapists prefer to call them unconstructive or maladaptive. Second, other people think that the word 'irrational' is being applied to them as individuals rather than to their beliefs. When these two misrepresentations are combined – i.e. when a person thinks that he is being told that he is crazy – then we have a powerful reason why the term 'irrational' is viewed as being pejorative.

Given that there are so many misconceptions of the terms 'rational' and 'irrational', RET therapists and trainers need to be vigilant when using them and to check carefully that the meaning that the words have in RET theory is accurately discerned by clients and trainees alike.

13 Putting the cart before the horse: the paradox of confidence, courage and comfort

Human beings frequently find personal change immensely difficult. As any counsellor knows, client change rarely occurs in a linear fashion and, particularly when faced with threat, clients will scuttle back to familiar, comfortable, but ultimately unproductive ways of coping. Helping clients to resist the lure of returning to cocoon-like, self-defeating patterns is a major task for counsellors and one that needs to be handled delicately. On the one hand, we can easily come adrift on the Scylla of not encouraging clients to resist the sirens of familiarity at all and yet, on the other, we can just as easily crash on the rocks of Charybdis by putting undue pressure on clients to resist the temptation of returning to the status quo. Yes, steering between Scylla and Charybdis is a tricky task and we need all the help we can get.

One avenue of help lies in understanding that change, by its very nature, involves clients moving away from familiarity into areas where they are *bound* to experience uncomfortable feelings which they need to tolerate or 'stay with' if they are to move on. Helping clients to understand this process *and* how they wittingly and unwittingly try to circumvent it, is so important that I would place it very high on any list of counsellor competencies that will no doubt be drawn up over the coming years.

One way that clients subvert the change process is by their beliefs about the conditions that have to exist before they initiate change. Three such beliefs frequently emerge in counselling and I want to focus on these in the remainder of this piece.

The first belief goes something like this: 'I can't do it [the desired activity] because I don't have the confidence to do it.' The problem with this belief is that it assumes that confidence has to come before action. This is patently untrue. How many of us were confident about driving before we got into a car for the first time? This issue leads me to recall when I undertook to overcome my anxiety about speaking in public due, in large part, to a bad stammer. I learned that I needed to speak up continually without confidence before I began to feel confident about public speaking. So, if clients want to develop confidence in something and they have some ability in that area, they need to do it unconfidently and keep doing it unconfidently until that confidence develops.

The second belief that blocks change is often expressed thus: 'I didn't have the courage to do it.' Again the assumption is that courage needs to be developed before carrying out an anxiety-related act. Research has shown that this is not true. People who have acted courageously cannot be discriminated from those who have not so acted by differing levels of fear. In fact, people who have displayed acts of courage are frequently surprised by their actions. When they are asked to explain why they acted as they did, they find it difficult to account for their behaviour. Certainly, they acknowledge that they were afraid before taking action – so fear hasn't stopped them from behaving courageously. When I embarked on my self-help programme to overcome my stammer-related anxiety, I was aware that I was fearful before I resolved to speak up in public gatherings. The point is that people rarely experience something called 'courage' before taking risks. This has been neatly encapsulated in the title of a recent self-help book by Susan Jeffers (*Feel the Fear and do it Anyway*).

The third change-impeding belief I want to consider here is often expressed thus: 'I didn't do it because I didn't feel comfortable doing it.' Once again the idea implicit in this statement is that a desired, but foreign, activity cannot be undertaken unless one experiences a sense of comfort first. The same argument applies here as with the previous two beliefs: in order to become comfortable doing something, one very frequently has to start off and continue to do it uncomfortably until the new behaviour becomes habitual and a new state of comfort is achieved. This is generally accepted by counsellors, although the belief is sometimes expressed by clients in ways that are more troublesome for some practitioners. Thus, some clients say: 'I didn't do it because it didn't feel right'; or 'I didn't do it because it didn't feel like me.' Those counsellors who have difficulty with such statements tend to subscribe to the idea that it is important for clients to 'feel and be themselves.' I sympathise with this view and would not suggest that a long-term goal of counselling is for clients to act in ways that are alien to them. But, and it's a big but, client change involves staying with the experience of 'feeling wrong' or 'not feeling like me' in the shorter term if new and more adaptive ways of being are going to be integrated into the self in the longer term.

Clients, then, often put the cart of confidence, courage and comfort before the horse of taking risks that can be change-enhancing. Our role as counsellors is to explain this to clients and to help them appreciate the paradox of personal change: that if you want to develop confidence, act courageously or be comfortable with a new way of being, you first need to do things unconfidently, uncourageously and uncomfortably.

Part IV

Ethical issues in counselling

14 Phony client, phony research

Many counsellors disregard the research literature on counselling. Some see many of the studies as being too far removed from real-life counselling to be of much practical value, while others have concerns about the ethical basis of much of the research. In this piece, I consider one study, the design of which raises just such ethical concerns.

P.G.K. Davies, in the July 1982 issue of the *British Journal of Guidance and Counselling*, reported the results of a pilot study which assessed ten telephone counsellors' responses to him as he role-played a 'client' who was supposedly under pressure by his family to get married. What he did was to write down the responses of the counsellors as he enacted his role, and then to analyse them according to a 5-point scale of facilitative counsellor responding. He found that only three of the ten counsellors responded at a level which (according to his scale) could be considered as facilitative. While it is important to study the quality of help offered by counselling hotlines, it is my view that Davies' approach was questionable on ethical grounds and that his results are accordingly open to a different interpretation.

My first criticism is that Davies deliberately deceived the counsellors into thinking that he was a 'real' client . He portrayed himself as a person in distress, when actually he was carrying out a research study and pretending to be a person in distress. It is therefore possible to conclude that most counsellors in his study offered poor counselling to a researcher playing a role. Even if we grant that most, if not all, of his 'subjects' were successfully deceived, to what extent are we as counsellors prepared to regard the results of transactions where one participant showed bad faith as representative of transactions where both participants show good faith? What is the generalisability of research findings that are based on inauthentic encounters such as those described by Davies?

First published in 1983.

This also raises a methodological point. The so-called high-level responses Davies mentions in his scale are based on the fact that counsellors must inevitably share his deception. A 'level 5' response, according to Davies, involves – among other things – the counsellor labelling and feeding back undercurrents not stated by the speaker. Surely an *accurate* 'level 5' response in the context of his study would not be 'Underneath what you say, you seem really angry' but 'Underneath what you say, you seem to be deceiving me'?

My second criticism concerns the fact that Davies did not obtain the informed consent of his 'subjects'. In most psychology experiments, subjects are at least invited to participate in a study. They are deceived as to the true purpose of the researcher, but are 'debriefed' after their participation has ended and the true purpose of the researcher is finally revealed. Davies neither invited counsellors to participate in his study nor debriefed them afterwards. If counselling researchers failed to obtain clients' informed consent and deliberately deceived them, I am sure that we would not read their report of such endeavours in the *British Journal of Guidance and Counselling*. Are counsellors less deserving of such ethical treatment?

It is important to study the quality of counselling offered by telephone hotlines. The question is, can we do so while gaining counsellors' informed consent, without employing deception and in a way in which the participating counsellors might benefit from the experience? I believe so. If I were conducting such a study, I would first contact the organisations concerned, openly disclose my purpose, and invite participation from organisational representatives and volunteering counsellors. I would stress that we would all need to collaborate on the enterprise and arrive at a methodology which would satisfy everyone's wishes: one which would help the organisation and participating counsellors to reflect non-defensively on any deficiencies in counselling skill that might be discovered, and one which would meet research criteria. Of course, the results of such research might have less external validity than Davies' findings but they would be obtained from 'good faith' transactions and thus would be more generalisable to similar 'good faith' transactions than are Davies' results.

Infallible research paradigms do not exist. Each paradigm has its strengths and weaknesses. But counselling research should be conducted in the spirit of counselling itself, with researchers offering counsellors the informed collaborative relationship, respect and authenticity that counsellors seek to offer their clients.

15 Confidentiality revisited*

Recently, a client of a psychotherapist registered a complaint against him in a newspaper article about the pitfalls of counselling. She had consulted this man with her mother and although the session was difficult she did consider that the therapist had suggested some valuable parameters by which they could usefully communicate with each other.

Five weeks later one of the woman's friends informed her that the therapist had, in the course of a newspaper column he writes, referred in detail to the session he had had with the mother–daughter pair.

Her mother also saw the piece and was distressed because of some derogatory remarks the therapist had made about her. Although she had thought the therapist had liked her, his comments led her to review this opinion.

In the original article, the daughter said that because of this episode she despaired of ever encouraging her mother to see another therapist. She contacted the therapist and complained about the discussion of their therapy session in his column. However, according to the woman, he was unrepentant, maintaining that the pair could not be identified from his description and denying therefore that he had done anything wrong.

He did offer them a free session to discuss the issue, but the woman declined this, wanting only an apology, which was not forthcoming.

The use of case material in publications on counselling and psychotherapy is a very delicate issue. On the one hand, practitioners and students of counselling do need case studies. They enliven and illustrate principles of practice and as such contribute to the education of workers in the field. However, protecting client confidentiality is paramount and one should not assume that past or present clients will not read case studies in even the most obscure professional publications.

First published in 1992.
*Please note that this article is published with the full permission of the clients referred to above.

As such, writers need to take great care in disguising material to protect the privacy of their clients. This can easily be done without losing the point that the material is used to illustrate. For example, the therapist above could easily have changed the gender and ages of the clients concerned. Identifying information that appeared in the therapist's newspaper article such as 'the daughter, now in her forties and happily married with children' could quite easily be altered significantly or omitted entirely without any loss to the thrust of the main argument. If it is at all likely that a client could be identified by a third party from the therapist's description or, as importantly, could recognise him- or herself, then the therapist should send the material to the client concerned and request permission to publish.

In the case discussed above, a number of these points were seemingly not attended to. The result was that the daughter's friend recognised the clients from the therapist's article, as could both the mother and daughter themselves. As the daughter said, '. . . the point is not whether other people could identify us, but that my mother and I recognised that this was our story, and it has harmed my mother greatly'. This harm was accentuated by the way in which the therapist referred to the interactive style of the mother. Imagine you are the mother as you read the following, 'While the daughter was speaking the mother was behaving like a manipulative, demanding child, ignoring what we were saying by poring over a diary containing incidents of alleged rejection'. How would you feel? Phrases like 'manipulative, demanding child' are bad enough when used in professional case conferences. When used in published form in a case which was readily identifiable by the people involved it is inexcusable. It not only reflects badly on the therapist in the case, it also fuels the fears of actual and potential clients that behind the caring façade, counsellors have sneering and pejorative attitudes towards them.

Most codes of ethics and practice address the issue of protecting the confidentiality of clients when discussing them in print. What this case shows is that we need to go further in our codes. We need to stress even more than we do the importance of disguising our clients' identities so that they cannot be recognised by themselves or by others. It also underscores the importance of requesting permission to publish when such identification is a possibility, however remote. To do otherwise is to risk causing clients the needless harm suffered by the mother and daughter as described above. I'm sorry the therapist in question did not admit his error.

16 Counselling, disclosure and the press

Soon after I had written 'Confidentiality revisited', a book purporting to tell the story of Princess Diana was published. In it, reference was made to a man who, it was claimed, had helped her deal with her problems over a lengthy period. On 5 July 1992, this man gave an interview to a national Sunday newspaper. In the article, he is described as 'her therapist' and as the man 'who has given the Princess massage and therapy at least once a week for the past three and a half years'. Leaving aside the thorny question of whether massage and counselling can be ethically combined within a given helping relationship, the interview and its aftermath raise important issues concerning the confidentiality of counselling and the press's understanding of it.

Now, it is clear from the interview that Diana's 'therapist' saw himself in a counselling role with her. In his own words, he claimed to provide 'a safe and effective framework within which the client can transform herself and improve her life'. I do not know what qualifications this man has, but the very fact that he was prepared to talk about his work with the Princess in the press contravenes any code of practice and ethics that I know of. It might be argued that the Princess had granted him permission to give the interview; after all it was said that she had implicitly allowed some of her 'circle' to talk to the author of the book mentioned earlier. However, most counsellors I know would not discuss easily identifiable details of a case with the press, even if given permission to do so by the client. We may write up cases for the professional literature with our client's permission, but we do so in a way that places the protection of the client's privacy above all else. So, by all the criteria I know of, Diana's 'therapist' acted unethically and unprofessionally by giving the interview to the Sunday newspaper.

What is the role of that newspaper in all this? By referring to the man as Diana's 'therapist', the author of the article clearly saw his

First published in 1992.

relationship with Diana as a professional one. Thus, she could have declined to publish the piece because it contained breaches of a client's confidentiality. That she did not is evidence either of ignorance of professional confidentiality or of complicity to breach that confidentiality.

Four days later, in a national daily newspaper, an article appeared which was, in effect, an exposé of Diana's 'therapist'. In the period between the two articles, the man had apparently been dismissed as her 'counsellor and masseur' – which tends to give lie to the argument that Diana had allowed him to disclose such personal details as the present state of her emotional health and her suitability for the work that they had embarked upon together. The author of this second article properly observed that 'no ethical therapist would disclose details of a client's sessions to a colleague, let alone a newspaper'. However, in her quest to expose the man, she disclosed the names of several of the man's former clients. Did they all give permission to be named? One could not, because she was dead, and it is not clear that the others did either. If they did not agree to be named, then this journalist is guilty, in my view, of invading their privacy. If they gave such permission, this should have been mentioned in the article so that there is no room for doubt. However, in my opinion, citing the names of these former clients, whether they agreed to be named or not, detracts from the main point of this article: that this man named a client in print and discussed her details with a journalist. The author of the second article goes on to discuss the 'therapist', using language which led him to instruct his solicitor to take legal proceedings against the newspaper. Whether this goes to court remains to be seen.

The point is that nobody comes away from this sad affair with much credit. The 'therapist' who disclosed details of his relationship with Diana, the Sunday newspaper reporter who wrote up the interview for publication and the daily newspaper journalist who disclosed names of some of the man's other clients – they are all guilty of soiling the sanctity of confidential therapeutic relationships.

So what can we in the counselling profession do when we consider that the press has, in one way or another, invaded the confidential nature of counselling relationships? We need to take action. We can write to editors of offending newspapers. We can make complaints to the Press Council. We can educate journalists about the ethics of our discipline and what constitute breaches of these ethics. If we do nothing, we may be shooting ourselves in the foot, because if we do not stand up to defend the professional nature of our work, nobody else will.

At the same time, we must ensure that our own house is in order. The person who purported to be Princess Diana's therapist is not a member of BAC, so our chief professional body has no disciplinary powers in this case. Is this another example of the need for a professional register of all practising counsellors? I suggest that you make your opinions known on this issue.

17 On advertising courses in counselling and psychotherapy

On a certain day in September 1992 there appeared in a national daily newspaper an advertisement for a one-year home study degree course in counselling skills which, it was implied, could lead to a career as a part-time or full-time psychotherapist. The course was offered by an organisation that I had never heard of (and neither, it turned out, had the United Kingdom Standing Conference for Psychotherapy (UKSCP)* or the British Association for Counselling).

I had reason to make a telephone complaint to the paper's advertisement department a year previously about a similar correspondence course run by a different organisation and received a letter confirming that that particular advertisement would no longer be accepted. However, following the appearance of the September advertisement, I decided to write to the newspaper's advertisement manager to request that the paper adopt a policy that ensures that it no longer advertises counselling and psychotherapy courses run by dubious organisations.

In my letter, I set out the steps that I believe every newspaper should adopt, protecting the public from the claims and practices of self-styled organisations and so-called 'experts'.

Step 1

There should be a small panel set up to 'vet' all advertisements offering courses in counselling and psychotherapy. I would be willing to convene such a panel, which would include representatives from major training and validating bodies in the field.

Step 2

When advertising copy is received by a newspaper, a member of staff should request full details of the advertising organisation or individual.

---

*Now the United Kingdom Council for Psychotherapy (UKCP).
First published in 1992 in modified form.

An organisation should be asked to submit its constitution, the code of ethics and practice under which its members and students practise and full details of its aims and activities. Those who run the organisation should be requested to submit CVs.

If these steps were taken I believe that neither of the advertisements would have appeared. In the most recent case, the details I received contained no information about the organisation and indeed promoted a course run by another 'college' and authorised by a third body. All the names have a plausible ring to them, but all are unknown to respected authorities in the field.

While nobody I consulted had heard of the designer or the principal tutors of the course, this is not, in itself, cause for alarm. However, I would be very interested to see their CVs to determine whether they have bona fide qualifications in the field of counselling and psychotherapy or whether, as I fear, their credentials derive from the self-same three institutions associated with the course.

Step 3

Prospective advertisers would have to submit details of their courses for scrutiny by the panel and only courses meeting proper standards of professional practice from bona fide organisations would be advertised.

As the course in question purports to train psychotherapists, it must be judged against generally accepted standards for psychotherapy training. In many respects, the details I received failed to meet such standards. The course did not screen applicants; previous, relevant experience was not required to enrol on the course; interviews were not held; and there was to be only minimal face-to-face contact between tutor and student, who was to receive six modules each comprising a video on 'insight into two techniques', certain reading material and assignments based on the foregoing. There was no face-to face supervision of any work done with 'patients' (their word) and no formal emphasis placed on the personal development of the therapist. Indeed, virtually every accepted canon of sound psychotherapy and counselling training was absent from the details I received.

Worse still, prospective students were told that they could begin to see 'patients' from the second month of the course and were informed that on completion of the course they would be awarded a 'Doctorate of Philosophy'. Students had to pay quite handsomely to enrol on the course (£1000–£1250) and various methods of payment were described in the details.

Let me end this piece with the final paragraph of my letter to the newspaper:

I hope I have made the point that I am extremely concerned that such courses are allowed to be advertised in your newspaper and I would be pleased to learn what checks you made on this particular organisation. I would also be interested to discuss with you the three steps I have described in this letter. . . Rather than help promote unprofessional and suspect training organisations, you have the opportunity not only to protect the public, but also to serve as the guardian of professional standards in this field.

As yet, the newspaper has not implemented a policy concerning the screening of advertising material, with respect to counselling and psychotherapy courses. Perhaps they need to look at the *Jewish Chronicle*, which does indeed ask to see advertisers' credentials, particularly if they are offering highly specialised qualifications and asking a lot of money for the privilege. Why should others not do this?

Part V

On clients

18 Bound but not gagged: a counsellor's dilemma

The dilemma that I wish to discuss has emerged from my work, still ongoing, with a married professional woman in her late thirties. I originally saw her together with her husband for conjoint marital therapy. They had sought such help at the husband's suggestion after many years of chronic marital discord. It transpired that Mrs D. had consistently resisted seeking help for their marital problems and the precipitating factor that led her to change her mind on this occasion was Mr D.'s visit to a solicitor to set the wheels of divorce in motion.

To put the case in context, Mrs D. had become, over a number of years, increasingly anxious about her husband going out in case he would not return. She was frightened that he might get killed in a car accident – some of their friends had died in this way – or that he would decide just not to return. If he returned home later than he had promised, his feeling was that he would be punished for this 'crime' for several days. Consequently he had decided to restrict his extra-domestic activities to a minimum for a few months before their initial consultation, when he decided 'enough was enough'. His position was that he couldn't stand the situation any longer and that his wife would have to change or he would go ahead with his petition for divorce. Mrs D. desperately wanted to preserve the marriage and agreed to attend conjoint sessions to attempt to change for the sake of the marriage.

I saw them for 15 sessions of marital therapy, an experience which was, quite frankly, very frustrating. They appeared to be locked into a rigid pattern and my therapeutic interventions had about as much impact as King Canute's efforts to reverse the incoming tide. At that point I offered them a number of alternatives: seeing another therapist for more marital therapy, or individual therapy with either me or someone else. I suggested that they consider what course of action they wanted to take, but in the interim a crisis occurred when Mr D.

First published in 1986.

returned to his solicitor and in response Mrs D. made a suicide attempt, after which she decided to come and see me for individual sessions. Meanwhile Mr D. sought another therapist for individual therapy.

It is here that my initial dilemma emerged. In discussing the suicide attempt with Mrs D. the following picture emerged. She had divorced her first husband primarily because he did not want children and she very much did. Mr and Mrs D. subsequently had two children (a boy aged nine-and-a-half and a girl aged seven). Mrs D. believes that it is crucial that their children are bought up by both parents. She further believes that while they would get over her death (i.e. her suicide) they would be traumatised by the constant reminder that their parents were not together should they divorce. Mrs D. believes that their children would suffer financially should they divorce and that the children's financial provision is a high priority for her. The couple are heavily insured and the husband and children stand to benefit considerably from her death. Thus Mrs D. is quite clear that if her husband pursues a divorce she will take herself off and kill herself.

Her reasons for coming to see me for individual therapy are because she believes it will help her to keep the marriage intact and to stop ruminating about matters. In the past she used to talk her concerns over with her mother, and this helped decrease her obsessive ruminations. Now her first objective cannot be achieved directly through therapy, because, in this instance, the decision to stay married or to divorce is largely in the hands of Mr D. However, the second objective can be legitimately achieved through psychotherapy and it was on this second basis that I agreed to see her – and yet I was not entirely happy doing so, because it was like accepting a contract to redecorate a house whose foundations were about to crumble away. I would ideally have liked Mrs D. to have the goal of pursuing as much happiness as possible even if her husband decided to divorce her, but she is just not interested in this goal. Should I, as her therapist, respect her choice or should I proceed in the hope that she might develop this goal as a result of our sessions? At the moment I feel bound by her limited therapeutic goals but I have not been gagged. Although she appears disinterested in living should her husband follow through on divorce proceedings, I have spoken up and tried to show her that her decision to commit suicide is based on false premises. I have tried to show her that she could live without her husband; that her children are more likely to be adversely affected by her suicide than by a divorce, particularly if the parent who leaves the familial home has ready access to them and sustains a friendly relationship with the divorced partner. So far this 'challenging' strategy has been to no avail. To what extent should I continue to challenge her on this point as opposed to acknowledging and going along with her and thus, as she would prefer,

rule the issue out of the therapeutic court? Now I believe that she does
have the right to take her own life, but I further believe that as a therapist (indeed as a member of society) I have the right to try to show her
that such a decision, in her case, is based on irrational thinking. It is
not as if she had an incurable disease and was in intolerable unceasing
pain. The potential for her to live a worthwhile life after divorce is
there. She, however, does not share my conviction.

I am fully aware that my 'challenging' strategy jeopardises the therapeutic alliance between us in that it is designed to achieve a goal that
she does not have. While I have chosen to be bound by her in that I
have accepted her limited goal of helping her to reduce her obsessive
ruminations, I refuse to be gagged by her and thus I keep trying to
widen her horizons.

In taking this course of action – and I do not wish to create the
impression I pursue this strategy in every session: I don't; I use it when
her suicidal ideation is prominent, which is closely linked to her husband's divorce-seeking behaviour – I am aware that I am adopting a
paternalistic stance towards her. What I am saying in effect is this: 'If
you would think rationally then you would see that life could be meaningful without your marriage. Your decision to kill yourself is thus evidence that you are not thinking rationally about this and I will
intervene if you threaten suicide.' Now the interesting issue here is that
I doubt whether I would pursue this 'challenging' strategy with her if
the stakes were not quite so high. If she had a particular phobia and
did not wish to discuss it with me, I would say: 'Fine, she could live a
worthwhile life with her phobia.' However, the stakes are high in this
case and she, from *my* perspective, is willing to forego a worthwhile
life. I think it is the issue of 'waste' that is the important one for me
here.

Indeed, I *have* intervened when, some months ago, she rang to
inform me that she would be leaving home the next day to kill herself.
(I had asked her to inform me if suicide was her intention, hoping to
have the opportunity to talk her out of it.) This episode was precipita-
ted by her discovery that there was another woman in her husband's
life. This relationship had started just before Mr and Mrs D. came into
marital therapy. This discovery brought matters to a head again. Once
more Mr D. went to his solicitor and once more Mrs D. threatened suicide. After I received her telephone call I rang her GP and informed the
duty social worker of my conversation with her. This culminated in a
late-night visit from a psychiatrist and the promise of a referral to a
local psychiatric clinic. Once again Mr D. backed down and the crisis
was, temporarily, over.

However, this 'Mexican stand-off' persists in the background and it
is difficult to see the end of it. I would take the same action if I received
a similar telephone call from Mrs D. However, the dilemma here is that

in doing so I am encroaching on her autonomy. The major function of making an intervention to stop someone from committing suicide is to enable them to reflect on the decision: indeed this is another reason I periodically challenge her on this matter. The more often I intervene and try to stop her committing suicide, however, the more I am encroaching on her autonomy and the less I am adhering to a therapeutic ideal: to promote rather than to inhibit a person's autonomy. So if this became a repeated pattern I would have to re-think my position, because the purpose of such intervention would then obviously not be to give the person time to reflect on her decision.

As an aside, if this did become an oft-repeated pattern one could legitimately enquire why Mrs D. would telephone me first. The reader may consider that Mrs D.'s suicide threats are designed to preserve her shaky marriage and that this gives her some power in her otherwise powerless position. I am certainly aware of this, yet I do not consider this to be her only motivation. I believe her when she says that she will kill herself in the final analysis. In a sense, I am falling back on the old adage used in other types of disputes, namely that as long as I can maintain 'talks' with Mrs D. there is some hope. Our therapeutic bond is not that strong, however, since she would stop seeing me tomorrow if her husband asked her to and if she thought that this request reflected hope for the preservation of her marriage.

How would I feel if she did kill herself while in therapy with me? This is difficult to answer. Part of my reason for continuing to take action to save Mrs D.'s life in the face of future suicide threats is because I want to protect myself. It is important for me to feel that I have done all I could to save her life. Since first seeing Mr and Mrs D. in conjoint marital therapy I have sought supervisory help on the case from several sources on many occasions. Thus I have acted in accordance with my professional code. Nevertheless, were Mrs D. to kill herself I would question myself quite keenly as, indeed, I have done throughout the case. Perhaps my handling of the marital therapy phase of treatment was poor? Perhaps I should have suggested referring them to a different therapist earlier in the marital sessions? However, I have to remind myself that I am not 'super-therapist'. I am a fallible human being struggling to do my best to intervene in a system that is quite resistant to change.

This case has also served to remind me of the limits of therapy – we just don't have magic bullets in counselling and psychotherapy. I am realistic enough to realise that the agendas with which Mr and Mrs D. entered therapy (and continue to have) are such as to defeat most therapeutic endeavours. (Mr D.'s hidden agenda: 'Change my wife, but I am to be allowed to do as I please. If this doesn't work, help me to leave this marriage without the blood of my wife on my hands'; Mrs D.'s overt agenda: 'Help me to preserve my marriage. If I have to

change I will do so only if my husband changes also'.) Perhaps I should
have extricated myself from this situation earlier. That would have
helped me but where would that have left Mr and Mrs D.? Trapped in
their misery with no-one to listen to them? Or would it have helped to
break the Mexican stand-off? And if so, what would have been the outcome? I presently feel as I imagine Mr D. feels – I am not prepared to
take the risk of extricating myself. So I remain bound but not gagged.

19 Officer, my client won't leave

I have always been an advocate of professional indemnity insurance. Most counsellors are highly professional in their dealings with their clients, but we can never be too careful because we can never predict with unfailing accuracy how some clients may view our best endeavours. In this piece, I want to relate an incident with a client which gave me a shock and over which I fretted for some time. To say that I was glad to have insurance is something of an understatement.

To protect the privacy of the client who I had seen only once before the incident in question, I have changed certain identifying details. The client rang me from a town in south-west England to make an appointment. I arranged to see her because she wanted specifically to consult a counsellor from the therapeutic tradition with which I am associated, there being no such counsellors in her locality.

Our first session was uneventful. She said that she could not attend sessions regularly as the distance between where she lived and I worked was too great, but indicated a wish to see me on an occasional, ad hoc basis. I agreed to this as I have made similar arrangements with a number of 'out of town' clients before, and it had always worked out quite well. In the session, I helped her to identify a number of self-defeating beliefs that were stopping her from reaching her goals and we discussed how she could go about changing them. She mentioned, in passing, that she had finished seeing a counsellor from a different tradition and that this contact had not been helpful. Again, it happens quite frequently that people consult me when they wish to see a practitioner from a different orientation than their previous counsellor when that contact has not proven productive. We discussed this briefly and nothing seemed untoward. After agreeing certain routine practicalities, the client left, seemingly satisfied. I had certainly no inkling about was to happen next.

About four months later, the client contacted me again for another session and again I agreed to see her. She arrived with a rucksack, a fact which did not strike me as being unusual at the time, as I assumed that she had just arrived and, it being late afternoon, had arranged to spend the night with a friend in London. Much of this second session was uneventful. We discussed her experiences of putting into practice what we covered in our first session and I made some suggestions as to how she could take things further. I also corrected one or two minor misconceptions that she had formed on a misunderstanding of material in one of my self-help books. She seemed quite satisfied and had obviously resonated with my approach. It was then that it happened. She began to get quite agitated when she spoke again of her previous counselling relationship. How could counsellors be allowed to practise an inferior approach, she exclaimed, when an obviously more effective approach (namely mine) was available? It was my duty to do something about it, she opined. Moreover, she would not leave my room until I had made a written undertaking to retrain all practitioners of the 'inferior' approach, apparently whether they wanted such retraining or not! I tried to empathise with her angry distress, and suggested that we deal with this issue at the beginning of our next session. She was immovable; unless, she reiterated, I gave her the written undertaking she sought, she would not leave my room and, pointing to her rucksack, she added that she was quite prepared to sleep in my office until I agreed to her demands. I could see that she meant what she said; so thinking on my feet, I replied that as the session had now ended and as she was refusing to leave, I considered that she was trespassing on my property. I would have no alternative, I said, but to call the police if she did not leave my office forthwith. 'Call the police, then' was her reply. Which is exactly what I did; we sat in absolute silence waiting for them to arrive. The police arrived after 20 minutes and evicted the client, saying that if she had a complaint against me, she should seek legal redress. She said that this was exactly what she intended to do and left peaceably.

When I recovered my composure – I was in a state of shock for about an hour – I telephoned my insurance agent and explained what had happened. He said that he would contact me in the morning after he had discussed the case with the insurance company. When he rang back he said that, while it was obvious that the client had no case against me, the insurance company strongly suggested that I have no further contact with her and, in the meantime, I was to write a full report on the incident just in case the client took her bizarre demand further.

As far as I am aware, the client did not take further action, although two years later she wrote me a very pleasant letter (which did not mention the incident at all), in which she stated that she wished to resume her therapy with me. I did not reply.

The work that counsellors do is stressful enough without incidents like this. While the vast majority of counsellors will never have to call the police to evict a client, who knows what will happen with the next new client who makes an appointment? You may never have to use professional indemnity insurance to defend yourself against a client's complaint, be it justified or bizarre, but if you're like me you'll appreciate having such insurance – just in case!

20 Oi, Windy! Over here

Counselling usually occurs within a specific context – normally the counsellor's room – and within an agreed specified time period – normally fifty minutes or an hour. In most cases, it is unlikely that counsellor and client will bump into each other between sessions, although this is more likely to occur where counsellors work in a setting shared by their clients (e.g. student counselling). What then should counsellors do when they *do* meet their clients in non-counselling situations? If you find yourself in the same supermarket lane, for example, or at the same party, what do you do? Do you wait for your client to make the first move? Do you go over and say 'hello'? Do you pretend that you haven't seen her (in this case) and act surprised if she says 'hello'? Or do you take the initiative and beat a hasty retreat, hoping that the client doesn't see you do so? If you do acknowledge one another, do you then go on to make small talk? Certainly, no counsellor with whom I conferred on this issue said they would discuss a client's personal concerns in such a situation, and most said that they would wait to be acknowledged by the client before giving their acknowledgement. Everyone that I spoke to said that they would not engage in small talk and all said that they would explore the significance of the chance meeting at the next counselling session. As one psychodynamic counsellor observed, such encounters are grist for the therapeutic mill.

Almost all the student counsellors that I spoke to said that the vast majority of their current clients choose not to acknowledge their presence. As one student counsellor graphically put it: 'I'm about as popular as the ECT therapist in *One flew over the cuckoo's nest*, when it comes to being acknowledged by my current clients.' This reluctance to acknowledge the presence of one's counsellor is most marked when the student client is with other people, for obvious reasons. 'I'm so well known on campus,' said one student counsellor, 'that showing that you know me is tantamount to admitting that you have personal problems.'

There's nothing unusual about the general position that counsellors take in dealing with chance encounters with their clients. 'Wait for your client to make the first move and if it is made, return the acknowledgement briefly and move on' seems to encapsulate this position in a nutshell. I see nothing to quarrel about here and, by and large, it also describes my practice. However, this position did nothing to prepare me for the chance meeting with a client I wish to discuss in the remainder of this piece.

The client was a young man in his early twenties who was referred to a local clinical psychology department where I do sessional work. The exact nature of his problem is not relevant to the incident, but what *is* relevant is that this problem was very distressing for my client. The client worked on a building site and was proud to be 'one of the lads'. He was ashamed not only of his problem, but also of his need to consult a counselling psychologist. During therapy he worked very hard and, after some difficult times and several setbacks, was able to control his disturbing thoughts. As he improved, we increased the length of time between sessions and finally agreed to meet every three months to check that he was maintaining his progress.

Two months after one of these follow-up sessions, I was making my way to the railway station at the end of a working day in the department. As I was walking past a nearby pub, I caught sight of my client having a drink with three other young men. It was a warm evening and the four of them were drinking outside. Having noticed my client, I averted my eyes as I assumed that he would not want to acknowledge me in the circumstances. How wrong I was. As I tried to make myself anonymous, my client recognised me and without a trace of self-consciousness shouted over to me: 'Oi, Windy! Over here'. To acknowledge him with a friendly nod and walk on may well have been the best course of action, if I had had the time to reflect. But I didn't have such time. I certainly did not anticipate his invitation and somehow to turn it down seemed churlish. So, warily, I went over to join them.

'Come and meet my mates,' said my client, and he proceeded to introduce me to them. 'This is Windy,' he said to his friends. 'He's my psychologist.' I was astonished. Not only had he chosen to acknowledge me in front of his mates, but he also considered that he could go as far as to introduce me to them as his psychologist. I felt really uncomfortable, too preoccupied with wanting to do the right thing from a professional point of view to appreciate what this meant for my client's progress. One of his friends offered to buy me a drink. This seemed to break the spell. To accept would have not been right, so I declined with thanks, bade farewell and left to catch my train.

A month later we had our next follow-up session and we discussed the incident. Apparently he had been genuinely pleased to see me, 'chuffed' that I had gone over to meet his friends, but understood fully why I didn't stop for a drink. He said that a few weeks earlier he had told his friends that he had been seeing a psychologist who had helped him to 'get his head straight'. He did not want to tell them in precise terms about the nature of his problem, but was pleased that he could be open about the fact that he had been seeing me. His friends were genuinely interested in what a psychologist did and this led to a general discussion of their various problems, both past and present. His friends were interested in meeting me 'in the flesh' and were amused to note my discomfort. 'He was a bit uptight, and him a psychologist, too,' one of them had observed.

Several counsellors with whom I have discussed this episode have ventured the opinion that my client's greeting and invitation were, under the circumstances, evidence of either drunkenness or a severe personality disturbance – the words 'borderline' and 'narcissistic' were mentioned in this respect. I think this is preposterous. What is more interesting is that I was so preoccupied by a desire to be a model professional that I did not realise the gains that my client had made which enabled him to greet me so unself-consciously and with genuine pleasure!

Part VI

Counsellor education and training

21 Counsellor training or counsellor education

Introduction

Those of us in Britain who are involved in the process of preparing people to work as counsellors tend to describe themselves as counsellor trainers. Our North American counterparts, on the other hand, tend to see themselves as counsellor educators. In this paper, I wish to consider the terms, 'counsellor training' and 'counsellor education' and ask the question: Are these similar or different activities? In addressing this issue, I solicited the views of ten leading British individuals who are well known for their work in training and/or educating counsellors. I will discuss these views, before considering some implications of the semantics of counsellor preparation.

Counsellor training and counsellor education: three views

In order to clarify the distinctions between 'counsellor training' and 'counsellor education', I carried out brief telephone interviews with ten of Britain's leading counsellor trainers/educators and there emerged three different ways of differentiating these activities.

View 1: level of activity

A view put forward by three of my respondents concerned level of activity. These respondents considered that 'counsellor training' is an activity engaged in at the 'Certificate' or 'Diploma' level of counsellor preparation, while 'counsellor education' occurs at the 'Masters' level. It is worthwhile pointing out that these respondents all work in institutions of higher education and are involved in preparing counsellors at both 'Diploma' and 'Masters' levels. It is also important to note that their 'Masters' students have to have prior training in counselling skills

First published in 1991.

in order to be eligible for the 'Masters' programmes, which do not themselves include substantial skills training.

View 2: Skills versus reflection

A second view concerned the content of the engaged activity. This view is similar to the first but differs in one important respect. While the first view distinguished between 'counsellor training' and 'counsellor education' by its focus on *level* of engaged activity, this second view differentiates the two activities with respect to their *content*. In this view, 'counsellor training' is basically concerned with the practicality of what is done or the acquisition and mastery of counselling skills (where such theory that is taught is in the service of skills training), whereas 'counsellor education' is concerned with helping students (through the study of a relevant knowledge base and through supervised practice) to become 'reflective practitioners' (Schon, 1983) who are able to work creatively with a broad range of clients and to reflect intelligently on that work. Again the assumption made here is that 'counsellor education' does not necessarily involve a substantive emphasis on skills training. This view was expressed by five of my respondents.

View 3: Skills versus skills plus reflection

The third view, which was expressed by two of my respondents, concerned the additive nature of 'counsellor education'. Once again the focus of 'counsellor training' is seen to be on the practicality of what is done or the acquisition and mastery of counselling skills. 'Counsellor education', however, involves focus *both* on skills *and* on other activities designed to facilitate the development of creative practice and intelligent reflection on that practice.

The impression I gained from conducting these interviews was that most of the respondents were content to consider themselves counsellor trainers for conventional reasons and that the distinctions they made between 'counsellor training' and 'counsellor education' were their initial thoughts on this subject. Thus, it is my hope that this article will initiate a wide-ranging debate on this issue rather than serving as the final work on the topic. Having said this, I wish to consider some of the implications that arise from this discussion of the semantics of counsellor preparation.

Implications

A number of the respondents reflected on why 'counsellor training' is so ubiquitous in British counselling and why 'counsellor education' is rarely used. Several considered that the term 'counselling training' is favoured because it highlights the vocational nature of counselling. In addition, the view was expressed that the term 'counselling training' demonstrates that counselling is a skilled activity and one which does not rely purely on the acquisition of theoretical knowledge.

One respondent, in particular, considered that the use of the term 'counsellor training' facilitates access of such training to suitable potential trainees who do not have the necessary academic qualifications to be admitted to programmes which may come under the rubric of 'counsellor education'. This opinion reflects the possible consequences of View 1 discussed above.

My own standpoint is in line with View 3, although I state my position with some degree of ambivalence. I agree with one of my respondents who argued that the accepted use of the term 'counsellor training' is indicative of a profession that has not quite come of age. If one considers medicine, dentistry, nursing, social work and education, it is striking that they all tend to use the term 'education' when referring to the preparation of students for entry to these professions. If counselling wants to consider itself a profession and to be viewed as such by the outside world then it will have to take its place alongside these other professions. Consequently, it will not only have to equip its professionals with requisite skills (what these skills are will, of course, depend on the approach to counselling being advocated), but it will also have to 'educate' these professionals in the disciplines that impinge upon the profession. Here I have in mind the disciplines of psychology, sociology, social anthropology, philosophy and comparative religion, among others. From this position 'training' (with its emphasis on skills) will either be an activity in its own right in the preparation of paraprofessionals or will form a part of the broader endeavour of 'counsellor education'. Professor Philip Gammage (personal communication) put this latter viewpoint well when he referred to training as focused on a set of skills embedded in education.

My ambivalence about this view is centred on the élitist, two-tiered structure to which it could (and probably would) lead. Namely, professional counsellors would graduate from 'counsellor education' programmes, schooled in both requisite skills and the cognate disciplines that impinge on the profession of counselling, while paraprofessional counsellors would graduate from skills-based 'counsellor training' programmes. This is not to say that professional counsellors would necessarily be more effective practitioners than paraprofessionals. Indeed, there is some evidence that they would not (Stein and Lambert, 1984). However, it would mean that professional counsellors would be better placed to benefit from any career structure that might emerge from the professionalisation of counselling.

This brings me to the final reason why I favour View 3. At present (to my knowledge) there are no departments of counselling in any institution of higher education in Britain. There are indeed no professors of counselling in Britain*. 'Counsellor training' programmes are found (usually on the periphery) in departments of psychology, applied social studies, adult education, to name but a few. Being on the periphery, these courses suffer from inadequate funding and limited promotion opportunities for staff. This is not a situation conducive to the health of a profession, and an ailing profession is ill-suited to argue the case for a career structure for its members. It is my belief that the establishment of 'counsellor education' programmes throughout Britain (as defined in View 3) will go some way to alleviate this state of affairs, particularly if they are comprehensive, known as 'education' programmes and based in departments of counselling in higher education institutions. If this move is supported by BAC so much the better. However, if the present situation (where 'training' rather than 'education' predominates) continues, then counselling as a profession may well be appropriated by the British Psychological Society, which is taking steps to lead to the establishment of chartered status for counselling psychologists. If this happens than one possible (albeit unlikely) consequence may be that it could be difficult for people to become counsellors without being chartered counselling psychologists.

I realise that I have strayed a long way from my original brief of distinguishing 'counsellor training' from 'counsellor education' and I recognise that the grim consequence I have outlined above is only one of a number of possible scenarios. However, I hope that this article will provide a catalyst for a discussion on the future of counsellor training/ education in Britain and thus on the future of counselling itself.

Acknowledgements

I wish to acknowledge the following people who kindly agreed to be interviewed for this article: Michael Carroll, Mary Charleton, Peter Cook, Emmy van Deurzen-Smith, Ian Horton, Dave Mearns, Pat Milner, Ellen Noonan, Brian Thorne and Sue Wheeler. I wish to make it clear, however, that only I am to be held responsible for the views put forward in this article.

References

SCHON, D.A. (1983). *The Reflective Practitioner: How Professionals Think in Action*. London: Temple Smith.
STEIN, D.M. and LAMBERT, M.J. (1984). On the relationship between therapist experience and psychotherapy outcome. *Clinical Psychology Review* 4, 1–16.

*There is now, me!

22 Training for the trainers of trainers of trainers. . . ?

The British Association for Counselling appears to be getting its professional act together. You can now become a BAC-accredited counsellor, a BAC-recognised supervisor and if you are a counsellor training course you can be recognised as kosher by BAC. Of course, you will have to meet the relevant *criteria* – which seems to be a popular word in BAC literature these days – and pay the relevant fee (which if you are a course is a tidy sum), but you will at least have the satisfaction of knowing that if you are accredited, recognised and (yes, this will ultimately come, folks) registered by BAC then all is right with the world. *Or is it*?

Now, don't get me wrong I'm not against all this professional flurry. Indeed, I'm a part of it. As my colleagues on BAC's Courses Recognition Group will testify I can be a real toughie, a mean man, for example, when it comes to spotting break times that are counted as course hours. However, when I am not caught up in all this activity, when I take a pause and reflect on the overall picture, I become uneasy. A rather nasty question keeps nagging at me. If I carefully formulate it, it is this:

> Are accredited counsellors who have trained on recognised courses and are supervised by recognised supervisors more helpful to their clients than non-accredited counsellors who have trained on non-recognised courses and are supervised by non-recognised supervisors?

Now I know that there are no studies that have addressed this question and I'm pretty sure that no-one in Britain would get the considerable research funds that it would take to begin to answer it. However, from what I know of the research literature on counselling and psychotherapy, I would be prepared to place a not inconsiderable wager that the answer would be a resounding *no*!

While I'm in a betting mood, I'd be prepared to place another wager. Namely, that the United Kingdom Standing Conference for

First published in 1991.

Psychotherapy* will ultimately be successful in instituting a register for psychotherapists. If they do, you will probably have to have a fairly lengthy personal therapy in order to get on the said register. 'Well, that's sensible,' I hear you say. Possibly, but again the research literature suggests that having had a personal therapy does not necessarily make you a more effective practitioner.

So, if clients do not recognisably benefit from these professional accoutrements, who does? The answer is: *we do*. The more counselling and psychotherapy are professionalised, the more status they will offer, and the more status there is, the more work there will be.

Look! I'm not advocating the abolition of the recognition of training courses, nor the abandonment of accreditation procedures. What I am voicing is a concern that the whole shooting match is in danger of getting out of hand and that great care needs to be taken that we don't fool ourselves that the rolling professional bandwagon is solely for the good of our clients. It isn't.

But I'll have to break off now. The doorbell has just gone and I have to supervise a trainee trainer of novice supervisors!

---

* Now the United Kingdom Council for Psychotherapy (UKCP).

23 What does the label stand for? An exercise in applied logic

When I had a viva voce for my MSc in Psychotherapy at Warwick University in 1980, one comment made by the external examiner struck me as very true and I have remembered it ever since. 'Think of designing a research study,' she said, 'as an exercise in applied logic.'

In my experience, many trainee counsellors have a decidedly negative attitude to counselling research. Part of this negativity stems, in my opinion, from fear – the fear of not being able to understand what researchers are saying – part stems from terror – the terror many feel when the word 'statistics' is uttered – and part stems from doubt – the doubt that what preoccupies researchers has anything meaningful to say to practitioners. If I am right about the widespread negative attitude towards counselling research among trainees, then it is up to counsellor trainers to rectify the situation.

In this piece I want to show how trainers can demonstrate to trainees that they can ask some very meaningful questions about the design of a research study by applying logic and in doing so can gain confidence in their ability to become sophisticated consumers of counselling research. It is my experience that an increase of such confidence leads to a more positive attitude towards this research. I will use the example of research designed to test the comparative effectiveness of two approaches to counselling to illustrate my point. In doing so, I will write as if I am addressing counsellor trainees directly.

Let us suppose that we are looking at a study which compared the effectiveness of rational–emotive therapy (RET) and gestalt therapy (GT) with students experiencing examination anxiety. Let us focus our attention on the two counselling approaches. What questions would you want to ask about their use in this study? I will focus most of my remarks on RET, although, of course, you will want to apply the same arguments when considering GT.

First, you would probably want to ask whether what has been labelled RET in this study really was RET. If you saw a bottle of perfume labelled 'Chanel No. 5' on sale cheaply, you would want to know that it was, in fact, that brand of perfume before you bought it. If so, do not assume that because the researcher has labelled one approach RET that it really is that approach. Do not, therefore, take the researcher's word for it. Ask whether he or she has demonstrated independently that the approach labelled RET actually constituted that approach. This is known as the *adherence* criterion. You will, in fact, need to be satisfied on two points here:

1. You will need to know the extent to which RET counsellors in the study performed behaviours that are *pre*scribed by RET.
2. You will need to know the extent to which RET counsellors in the study did not perform behaviours *pro*scribed by this counselling approach.

Let us suppose that the researcher has devised a scale to measure RET adherence which includes items that cover both positive and negative adherence. She validated this scale by giving it to a panel of RET experts. Satisfied that she had developed a valid scale of RET adherence, she administered it to the RET counsellors employed in this study, asking them to mark the extent to which they performed behaviours in the study as indicated on the scale. What has the researcher discovered by such a method? Remember, this is an exercise in applied logic. The researcher has collected data on the counsellors' descriptions of what they did. Is this good evidence that they *actually* performed those behaviours in the study? Of course not. Now, let's suppose that the researcher had chosen RET counsellors on the basis that they had *actually* demonstrated RET adherence in a pre-study screening exercise. She did this by having independent and informed judges listen to and rate audio tapes of the counsellors' practice of RET with exam-anxious students prior to the study that we are considering, and those who met the adherence criterion were selected for the study. What does this tell us? Well, it tells us that the RET counsellors employed in the study had met the adherence criterion in one setting and this is, of course, an improvement over the counsellor self-report exercise described earlier. But is it foolproof? No, it is not. Just because the counsellors had demonstrated adherence in one setting, it does not necessarily follow that they demonstrated adherence in *this* study. So what should the researcher have done? She needed to have tape-recorded all the counselling sessions carried out in her study and should have had at least two independent and expert judges listen to a sample of these sessions and rate them on a valid and reliable RET adherence scale. A previously established cut-off point of adherence should have been set, and if both judges agreed that all RET counsellors met this criterion then, and only then, can we say that what has been labelled RET in this study actually is RET.

I have dwelled at length on the adherence issue to demonstrate how logic can be applied to the business of appraising one aspect of a research design. In fact, there are three other questions we need to ask our researcher about the counselling approaches in her study. These relate to: purity, differentiability and quality. I will consider each very briefly.

Purity

We need to ask our researcher how 'pure' the approaches used in her study were. Even if both RET and GT met the criterion of adherence, they may have differed in purity. A measure of purity can be gained by considering the proportion of approach-consistent behaviours to total counsellor behaviours. The larger the resultant proportion, the 'purer' the approach.

Differentiability

We need to ask our researcher whether the two counselling approaches in the study were able to be differentiated. Here, tapes of both RET and GT from the study could be played to judges not told which approach they were listening to, with the purpose of determining the extent to which the two approaches could be told apart.

Quality

Here, we need to know how *well* each approach was practised. Quality ratings could be made at the same time as adherence ratings, although to be rigorous it would be better to use a different set of judges, as there could be a tendency for the same judges to rate high-adherence RET as good quality RET. The two criteria are, of course, different. Just because RET in the study has been identified as RET (adherence) does not necessarily mean that it will be rated as good RET (quality). The use of separate raters here doesn't muddy the waters.

Now, if it could be demonstrated that both approaches had equally high adherence ratings, were equally pure, could be differentiated from each other and were considered to be of equal high quality, we can be sure that a valid comparison was being made with respect to the independent variable in the study, i.e. RET versus GT. There are other questions that need to be asked of our researcher – e.g. were both approaches equally credible to the clients in the study? – but that takes us beyond the scope of this short piece. If, however, the approaches differed in levels of adherence, purity and/or quality, any variation in outcome cannot properly be attributed to their differing effectiveness with students experiencing exam anxiety, as the results could just as easily be due to dissimilarities in one or more of the levels previously mentioned.

The point I want to reiterate, then, is that trainee counsellors do not need a detailed knowledge of research design or statistics to evaluate the way a piece of research has been carried out. What they *do* need to do is to apply logic to their appraisal. I have no doubt that they can do this, as I know of no evidence to show that trainee counsellors are less logical than any other group of students. This, despite protestations to the contrary, from those who consider counsellors to be wishy-washy, unscientific romantics!

24 Personal therapy: mandatory or recommended?

The question I wish to consider here is: should personal therapy be a mandatory part of counsellor training? The reasons for it being a course requirement are well rehearsed in the literature, but they bear repetition. The first reason is that it is essential for trainees to know what it feels like to occupy the client's chair. Doing so, it is argued, encourages trainees to understand the hopes, fears and other feelings that their own clients are likely to have in the counselling process. This empathy, it is claimed, will help them be more in tune with their clients and will make them more effective practitioners as a result.

The second reason that is given in favour of mandatory personal therapy is that it will help trainees to confront and deal with their own personal problems. If these problems are not resolved adequately, then they will intrude into the counselling process either by way of negative countertransference reactions or by dint of distracting the counsellor from giving the client undivided attention.

The third reason that is advanced in favour of personal therapy, although not necessarily in favour of it being a mandatory part of training, is that it gives trainees first-hand exposure to good therapeutic practice. Working with a talented therapist brings alive, in a personal and immediate way, some of the theoretical and practical concepts that trainees are taught on their courses. In therapy, they do not just learn *about* transference, for example, they *experience* it. As such, the concept becomes personally meaningful and will be better integrated into the trainee's understanding of the counselling process than it would if it were just grasped intellectually.

I would not disagree with these reasons if it could be shown that personal therapy made a difference to client outcome. We have a wealth of data to show that trainees and more experienced counsellors value their personal therapy and consider the experience to have enriched their own practice of the craft of counselling. In fact, I have conducted such research myself. However, I do have some lingering doubts about such evidence. Having committed oneself to the profession of counselling and to the not inconsiderable expense of personal therapy, it may induce a very uncomfortable level of cognitive dissonance to admit to oneself and to others that one's personal therapy was not a beneficial experience. Making such an admission may lead one, for example, to begin to doubt one's own suitability for the field or, if one lays the blame for this less than salubrious experience at the therapist's door, one would have to confront the difficult realisation that one had paid quite a lot of money to this inept individual. As I say, these are lingering doubts, but they will not go away.

What would help to silence these doubts would be hard data that personal therapy actually made trainees more effective practitioners than trainees who had not received such therapy and (as I said before), as far as I'm aware, we have no such evidence (nor, to be fair, do we have evidence to the contrary). My friend and colleague, John Norcross, who has a research interest in this area, acknowledges that we have no hard evidence that personal therapy makes a positive difference for client outcome, but that does not concern him as much as it does me. He says that the relationship between personal therapy and therapeutic outcome for clients 'is probably strong, but we will never discern it given our conventional research designs'. He notes that given the difficulty in evaluating psychotherapy outcome and the huge number of therapist variables which impact on outcome, we should not expect a strong and consistent relationship between personal therapy and client outcome to show up in the research literature. The relationship is, he concludes, a matter of faith.

Interestingly, Norcross does not think that personal therapy should be mandatory for trainees, which seems to him authoritarian. I would concur. I do not like the mandatory feel of insisting that trainees should all have personal therapy, partly because I consider that therapy, in all its forms, should be undertaken voluntarily and partly because I am not convinced that personal therapy (as it is currently conceived) makes a real difference to client outcome. So let me outline my position on this difficult topic.

1. Trainees should ideally commit themselves to some ongoing personal development work during training. This may encompass such diverse activities as personal therapy, co-counselling and outward bound courses. Trainees should be free to choose the activity or activities that best enhance their exploration of themselves. Potential applicants who have no interest in self-exploration should be rejected.
2. Trainees who have not had personal therapy before should be encouraged, but not forced, to enter such therapy. Trainers should discuss the three reasons usually given for it being a mandatory part

of training and indicate that it may be in their interests to be in personal therapy at some point in their careers – there is some evidence that not having had personal therapy is viewed negatively in the field. However, these arguments should be presented factually and trainees left to make their own decision on the matter.

3. Trainees who have had personal therapy before the start of a training course should be encouraged to continue with it if they wish to. I consider the idea that trainees ought to be in personal therapy during a course even though they have had extensive therapy beforehand and no longer require it, to be a ridiculous and tyrannical one.

4. The relevance of personal therapy to counselling practice needs to be increased. What I have in mind is something akin to what happens in unilateral couple therapy where the focus of the work is on the couple even though only one member of the dyad attends. In practice-focused personal therapy, as I call it, trainees would explore the personal issues that their work with clients has triggered, but the resultant exploration would always be linked to clinical work. It may be that one of the reasons why personal therapy has not been found to be more strongly associated with client outcome in the research literature is that such therapy, as it is currently conceived, is too general and wide-ranging in its focus. Perhaps increasing its direct relevance to practice will make a difference in this respect.

At present I do include personal therapy as a mandatory element on the MSc Counselling course that I direct. I do this not out of a strong conviction of the efficacy of such therapy, but because I do not want my trainees to suffer later in the market place by not having been in personal therapy during their course. After writing this, I realise that I am wrong. In future, I will outline the arguments and allow trainees to choose for themselves. What better course of action for a counsellor trainer?

25 A consumer's guide to counselling skills courses

Everywhere you look these days, someone seems to be running a course in counselling skills. These range from a one-day taster to a two-year comprehensive grounding in the subject. In this age of quality assurance, how is one to judge if the course one is considering joining, or indeed has joined, meets minimum standards of quality? This question is at present being considered by a working party of the BAC's Course Recognition Group and in due course this body will present its recommendations. In the meantime, let me outline some guidelines for those confused by the plethora of training opportunities in this area. I address my remarks to substantial skills training courses, although they also apply to short courses, as long as these courses seek to teach and have trainees practise counselling skills.

The first question to ask about a course is whether the skills being taught on it are presented in a coherent way. Here, a clear rationale for the skills needs to be presented, and the whole enterprise should be based on a clear, well-articulated philosophy of helping. This latter criterion is important to enable potential or actual trainees to judge whether or not what's on offer has relevance to their work situation and/or training needs.

The second question to ask concerns methods of teaching. Here, skills courses should ideally offer six ingredients.

First, each skill needs to be clearly delineated and its purposes made clear. Guidance should be offered with respect to when the skill should be used and, as importantly, when it should *not* be used.

Second, clear models of good and bad practice with respect to the skill should be demonstrated so that trainees are given clear information concerning what to do and what not to do. Here, the skill should be modelled by a tutor or should be demonstrated using audio or audiovisual materials.

Third, ample opportunity to practise the skill should be given and trainees should be observed using the skill by someone informed in its use. This is, of course, one of the tutors. While I have no objection to another trainee observing a colleague's performance (as often happens when triads are formed), unless the trainee in the role of counsellor is also observed by a tutor, informed feedback cannot be given. It is also important for all trainees to be given the opportunity to practise each skill and for all to be observed by a tutor. Observation can be done live or delayed if audio or video tapes of peer counselling practice are employed. If the latter are used, the period of delay between skill practice and skill observation should be kept to a minimum.

Fourth, informed feedback should be given to each trainee. I stress the importance of informed (i.e. tutor) feedback here, because it is unrealistic to expect such feedback from fellow trainees. While they may well have something valuable to contribute to the feedback process – the observer may well notice something that the tutor didn't and the trainee in the role of client can say what it felt like to be counselled by the 'counsellor' – there really is no substitute to receiving feedback from someone who is herself skilled, knows what to look for and can give constructive comment on what she has observed. The way feedback is given is, of course, very important. My own experience is that trainees benefit most when the tutor comments on what the trainee did well and on what he needs to improve. Feedback needs to respect the integrity of the trainee and it should be made clear that comment is being made on skill performance not on the worth of the person. Despite this, some trainees upset themselves even at the gentlest suggestion that they could improve their performance (especially when this is done in front of other course members) so that great care must be taken by all concerned in the feedback process. Finally, as with the practice–observation part of the training sequence, any delay between observation and feedback should be kept to a minimum.

Fifth, a trainee needs to repeat the practice–observation–feedback sequence until reached a minimum level of competency at using the skill in question has been reached. A trainee will only reach competency level when he or she has demonstrated competence! Expecting that he will do so after receiving even the most excellent feedback, without putting this feedback into effect is, I argue, unrealistic.

Sixth, particular care needs to be exercised when the stage of combining skills is reached. If possible, this should be done in a graded, additive fashion to avoid trainees becoming overwhelmed at the enormity of the task of 'putting it all together'. How this is best done is beyond the scope of this short piece. The point I want to emphasise here is that trainees should satisfy themselves that attention is paid to this important, albeit advanced stage of the skills training process.

The third question to ask of a training course concerns the qualifications of staff and the size of staff:student ratios. Believe it or not, I have heard that on some courses, tutors have not themselves received extended counselling skills training! Clearly this is unacceptable, so do not be afraid to enquire about the qualifications and experience of staff. Now, of course, a trainer has to get her experience somewhere. As long as she has had extended training and substantial experience in using the skills in a relevant setting, the use of a trainee skills trainer on courses is acceptable as long as her performance is being monitored directly by a senior trainer. If this is the case it should be made explicit at the outset to trainees.

Now we come to the trickiest question of all – that of staff:student ratios. If you have carefully read the section on training methods, you will have quickly discerned that counselling skills training does not lend itself to large staff:student ratios. An ideal ratio would be one tutor to between four and six students. However, we live in far from ideal times and both educational institutions and training organisations would have to charge prohibitive fees to accommodate this piece of Dryden fantasy. However, any ratio bigger than 1:12 makes counselling skills training unworkable (and even this is pushing it). Maybe there are skills trainers who can do an excellent job with even bigger ratios – if so, I'd like to meet them. Perhaps the best advice I can give is this: enquire of tutors (and past students, who may give you more reliable information) how much individual time you will get practising each skill and how much tutor feedback you will be given. Really try to pin the tutor down. Shop around until you find a course that will give you sufficient individual attention, and if the course adheres to the competency-based model of training, so much the better.

I hope you find this advice helpful. If any of you wish to write to me concerning your experiences on an extended counselling skills training course, I'd like to hear from you. A consumer's guide is of little value without feedback from the consumer.

Part VII

Personal experiences and reflections

26 Voluntary redundancy and beyond: a counsellor trainer's odyssey

In this paper I wish to outline my experiences since leaving my university position at the University of Aston in Birmingham in July 1983 and to discuss some of the issues that emerged from taking such a decision. I will start, however, by covering the background to my decision to take voluntary redundancy. It is now well known that Aston University received a 31% (approx.) reduction in its UGC funding in the early 1980s. What is less well known is the impact that this had on the Department of Educational Enquiry which ran the well-established one-year Postgraduate Diploma in Counselling and Educational Settings course on which I served as Course Tutor from 1977 onwards. Before the 'infamous' UGC letter was received by Aston University, the Department of Educational Enquiry was a thriving department of sixteen staff whose research output was second to none in the University. The Department ran two postgraduate courses and a very successful new (at that time) undergraduate course in human communication. As a result of the internal wranglings prompted by the UGC letter, the Department of Educational Enquiry was given a target of reducing its staff from sixteen to six It achieved this only after a number of established staff took early retirement or opted for one of the voluntary redundancy schemes that were quickly put on offer at the University.

After the department achieved its target of six staff, it was then subjected to an independent external review, the result of which was that it was deemed to be 'too small' to sustain meaningful educational activities. At this point staff were interviewed by the Vice-Chancellor and offered a new home. I was offered the opportunity to join the Manpower Management and Legal Studies Group of the Management Centre, a decision that was greeted with a great deal of puzzlement by both myself and the staff within that group. At that time the responsibility for running the counselling course was transferred to the

First published in 1985.

Management Centre, the immediate effect of which was that all secretarial assistance was stopped and I was left with the daunting task of running the counselling course with no secretarial assistance and no support from the Management Centre which, while promising much, delivered little in real ongoing support. I was also forced to pay for secretarial help out of my own pocket. It appeared to me that my long-term prospects at the University were rather bleak, given that there were very few people interested in counselling within the Management Centre and that there were signs that the nature of the counselling course would soon be changed to fit in more with the ethos of that part of the University. A new redundancy scheme was introduced at that time whereupon members of staff could receive a lump sum of £26 000, so I decided to accept voluntary redundancy, particularly as I was also offered the inducement to return the following year to teach on the counselling course on a part-time basis. I left full-time employment at the University in July 1983 having tried to ensure that the appropriate office in the Management Centre would ensure that the following year's Diploma students would receive proper tutorial assistance.

In retrospect I consider that my return to Aston University on a part-time basis in October 1983 was a mistake. I found it much more difficult than I expected to cope with the tension of becoming an external part-time lecturer where before I had been centrally involved in the Course as a Course Tutor. I was caught between the two horns of a dilemma – on the one hand I wanted to intervene as I was dissatisfied that the students were, in my opinion, being neglected to some degree by the Management Centre and, on the other hand I was aware that making such an intervention was not my paid responsibility. Also, since a new Course Tutor had been appointed to the Course it seemed best for me to keep out of internal University affairs. I was unable to solve this dilemma successfully and tended to wander between the two positions over the course of that academic year.

Also, as part of my 'leaving package', I joined a career-counselling programme offered by a private consultancy firm who were contracted to Aston University to offer people who had accepted voluntary redundancy an opportunity to explore their future career prospects. I decided to undergo this programme partly out of interest, partly because it was free and partly because I thought it might provide real assistance in helping me to re-launch my career. At this time I was confident that I would not be out of a job for too long. I predicted that a person with my academic qualifications, training and clinical experience would not find it very difficult to find another full-time position. At that time I was quite hopeful that by the time my part-time contract with the University of Aston had ended in June 1984 I would have found a new job, although I was not sure whether this would be within academia.The career counselling package was of some use in helping me to clarify what I did not want to do, but in some respects it was counter-productive in that I was encouraged to develop highly polished professional CVs which may have gone down well in the industrial world but, as I subsequently discovered, were not very well received by academic institutions and by agencies that were concerned with training counsellors or offering counselling services. It also gradually became clear to me that my original prediction of a quick return to full employment was extremely over-optimistic and I was beginning to adjust myself to the idea that I would join the dole in June 1984, which I did.

I remained unemployed from June to November 1984, thereby qualifying to be accepted by the Government's Enterprise Allowance Scheme which offers a financial inducement to people to set up in self-employed businesses – an inducement which was more financially rewarding than remaining on the dole. Under the Enterprise Allowance Scheme I formally set up my own Consultation and Training business in Counselling Psychology in November 1984. However, from the outset I had considered this to be a temporary measure until I had gained another full-time position. This I obtained in March 1985 when I was appointed Lecturer in Psychology at Goldsmiths' College, University of London, a post which I took up in August 1985.

From the time I left Aston University in July 1983 until I was appointed to my post at Goldsmiths' College in March 1985, I made 55 job applications. An analysis of these job applications and the posts for which I was interviewed are presented in Table 26.1.

Table 26.1 Analysis of job applications and interviews (July 1983–March 1985)		
	Number of applications	*Number of interviews*
Lectureships (counselling; psychology)	13	6
Practitioner posts	15	6
Administrative positions (in the helping professions)	10	3
Training posts	3	0
Research posts	1	1
Clinical psychology courses (applying as a student to be retrained)	13	5
Total	55	21

Generally speaking, my experiences of making applications and being interviewed for jobs in the field of counselling and related posts indicated that it is quite rare for a person in my position to receive reliable feedback concerning the suitability of his or her applications and why they had failed. However, it is fair to say that I stopped making such enquiries after a while because very few institutions or organisations seemed to demonstrate a sensitive or caring attitude to me as an interviewee (a notable exception here was the Student Counselling Service at the University of Lancaster, who conducted themselves in a thoroughly dignified, professional and empathic manner consistent with the profession of counselling). Indeed, I had a number of rather unpleasant experiences. For example, at one College of Further Education interviewees were not even offered a cup of coffee during an interview process which lasted the whole day, but were shown to a coffee machine and told that it took ten pence pieces. Perhaps my most discouraging experience was being interviewed for a lecturing position in counselling at an Institute of Higher Education who decided not to appoint any of the three candidates. We were invited down to the Head of Department's room and told that none of us had sufficient teaching experience to merit being appointed at Lecturer II level, although it was hinted that should any of us consider accepting the post at Lecturer I level, this might be a possibility! Considering my experience as a lecturer and counsellor trainer this was nothing short of insulting.

During the two-year period between leaving my post at Aston and obtaining my new post at Goldsmiths' College, it seems to me that I coped rather well with the experience. It is important to note at the outset that I did not experience any financial problems during this period since I had invested my lump sum of £26 000 from Aston University and was living off the interest. In addition, my wife had a full-time teaching job in Birmingham during that period.

On the personal side I was able to apply the principles of rational–emotive therapy to my situation. I was never depressed during this period and firmly accepted myself for being out of a job and, in fact, frequently reviewed my strengths particularly after failing to be appointed for one of the 20 interviews that I attended without success. Later I did receive helpful feedback that what I construed as displays of self-confidence at interviews were perceived as arrogance, and it is interesting to note that I was appointed at an interview at which I felt most anxious! I was occasionally destructively angry, particularly about the treatment which I received at the Institute of Higher Education mentioned earlier, but I was eventually able to show myself that although I considered that I deserved better treatment, that did not mean that the staff concerned *had* to treat me well at the interview, although I very much preferred this. Interestingly enough, although occasionally I did consider that I would never obtain another job again, most of the time I did not waiver in the belief that eventually I would find a job to which I could commit myself and I always considered the self-employed option as temporary. In summary, I consider that I coped rather well with my plight and did not feel the need to have personal counselling for myself. Although I was able to bring my own personal coping resources to the situation to good effect, I was able to draw upon the caring support of a number of important people in my life. In particular, my wife Louise was incredibly supportive and accepted the pace of life that I chose to live during this two-year period. I also found it particularly helpful that my family and friends did not constantly ask about the progress of my job applications and trusted me to tell them what I wanted to tell them. It is interesting to note at this point that a number of people of my acquaintance in the counselling profession seemed to find it rather difficult to refrain from attempting to counsel me, a service I certainly did not require from them at that time! On reflection I consider that one of the most therapeutic activities that I was engaged in during this period was my writing. Indeed, the two-year period to which I refer was the most productive and creative period in my professional life, although, of course, I certainly had the time to devote to my writing activities. Writing for me was important for two reasons: first, it enabled me to become involved in something creative; and secondly, it enabled me to feel that I was making a contribution to the profession which I never felt that I had left. In conclusion I would say that the period from accepting voluntary redundancy to taking up my post at Goldsmiths' College could be encapsulated in the phrase: 'It was a valuable experience, I'm glad I had it, but I wouldn't like to have it again!'

27 Keep going, take a break or give up?

As most readers may know I write and edit books on counselling and psychotherapy. In fact, February 1992 marked the publication of my 50th book. I really enjoy this activity and I think I'm pretty good at it. Like all writers, I publish because I think I have something to say and because I assume that there is a market for the works that I produce. Indeed, the vast majority of the books that my name is associated with have enjoyed favourable reviews. However, recently I have heard and read comments of my publishing activities that have made me pause for thought. I have begun to wonder how widely held the views encompassed in these comments (which I discuss below) are. So what I want to do in this column is to tell you, the reader, about these comments and give you the opportunity to share your views with me via *Counselling News*.

Let me start with the published comments. The most attacking comment that has appeared in print was made by the book review editor of the *Bethlem and Maudesley Gazette*. In his review of one of my books, he refers to me as 'the Barbara Cartland of the counselling world' and while he concedes that my works have merit, he opines that none of my books is that special. In conclusion, he suggests that I declare a four-year publishing moratorium before coming back to write the definitive book on counselling.

In another review of a different book, my friend and colleague, Colin Feltham, referred in passing to the 'Drydenisation' of counselling, a kind of one-man take over of the counselling literature. Now both of these reviewers have a point. I don't regard any of my books as classics; valuable, yes, but classics, no. And while I have no intention to 'Drydenise' anything, I can see why Colin came to use this striking term. In fact both of these points were summarised, rather cryptically, by a colleague at Goldsmiths' who, while discussing the publishing profiles

---

First published in 1991 in slightly modified form.

of members of the Psychology department, referred to me as the Macdonalds of the department

Now the verbal feedback. I'll leave aside the comments of those who have speculated on the vast wealth I have accumulated from my books. As any author or editor of academic books will tell you, the financial return from our endeavours is puny. In fact, I have likened the financial relationship between academic publisher and writer as akin to pimp and prostitute and I'll leave you to guess which is which. All I can say is that I'm *not* writing this from my yacht! No, the verbal comments to which I refer also pertain to the volume of my publishing efforts. Here are some of them: 'Not another bloody book from Dryden', 'Not another book from bloody Dryden', 'Don't you care about the rain forests?', 'Are you trying to start the Dryden book of the month club?'.

Now some or even most of these comments were made in good humour. But these comments are beginning to proliferate and no doubt as more of my books hit the shelves, the more they will be voiced.

My concern is how widespread are these views. This is where you come in. Please write in and tell me if you think I should (1) keep going (my books are valuable); (2) take a break (I've gone stale); or (3) give up (my books aren't valuable). Also please feel free to elaborate on your 'vote' on a separate piece of paper. A free annual subscription to the magazine will be given for the best supporting statement in each category and these will be published in *Counselling News*, as will the result of the poll.

I won't promise to be guided by the decision, but it will provide me with most useful feedback as I attempt to make sense of the comments I have discussed with you here. I want to keep publishing, but if my efforts are not generally appreciated, I need to take that into account. Thank you in anticipation.

Postscript

The response to the survey was as follows: nineteen people took part: eleven encouraged me to continue, three wanted me to take a break, one wanted me to give up, one didn't know and two suggested that I should do what I want. Finally, one wrote a very long letter, but seemed to have no firm opinion. A prize was awarded in each of the three nominated categories.

28 Specialists, all-rounders and pigeon-holes

At the end of a lecture that I gave recently, I asked the audience to write down questions on the theme of 'everything you have always wanted to know about counselling, but were afraid to ask'. I told the audience that they could address their questions either to a named individual (including myself) or in general. One question that was addressed to me personally was as follows: 'Due to you being so busy with the theoretical aspects of counselling and writing many books, do you ever feel that you're becoming distant from the focus of counselling, i.e. the client?'

This question stayed with me for a number of days, niggling at me, until I realised what it reminded me of. It made me recall the time when I was out of work and attended interviews for a veritable plethora of counselling and counselling-related posts, all of which I failed to obtain. While it is notoriously difficult to receive reliable feedback on one's performance at interview, the sense I got was that I was being pigeon-holed. Interviewers for the academic posts that I applied for saw me as a clinician; boards that were considering me for counselling practitioner posts viewed me as an academic and those wondering whether or not to appoint me for the more administrative positions judged me to be either an academic or a practitioner. When I argued that I considered myself a good all-rounder, I was written off as arrogant. If the British don't like people who proclaim specific talents, they *really* don't like those who describe themselves as good all-rounders.

This is what the question stirred up in me, for if you read it again, you will see that the enquirer makes an assumption that because I write and edit many books I have necessarily become distant from clients, by which I assume the questioner means either that I do not counsel clients at all or that I do so very infrequently. Actually, nothing is further from the truth. In an average week I see about twenty individual or couple clients and run a group. If that is becoming distant from clients, I plead guilty, but I have the sense that my questioner may well be surprised by my response. Personally, I would find it difficult to write as much as I do without this ongoing experience. Indeed, the idea that I (or anyone else) could legitimately train counsellors without actively working with clients at the same time is one that I have always scorned.

So what is my professional self-view? I see myself as a good all-rounder in the field of counselling. I have some talent as a practitioner, a trainer and a supervisor; I'm good at writing clear and accessible texts for counsellors, and very good at conceiving and producing edited texts and book series on counselling and psychotherapy. I would further say that I'm an average researcher, preferring to be an up-to-date consumer of the research literature rather than an active contributor to it.

Now, I'm well aware that by going into all this I am setting myself up for a variety of other criticisms; for example 'he's a jack of all trades and master of none' or 'he's a one-dimensional person whose whole life is devoted to counselling'. I'm not really that concerned if such criticisms do come my way. What I *am* concerned about is to dispel the idea that I am distant from clients, for that is patently not true and casts aspersions on the validity of my writings. For while I may seem from the outside to be an academic specialist, I hope I have shown this to be false. I am writing in this vein not to knock specialists, but to give a plug for the much misunderstood, much maligned all-rounder. I also wish to warn against the dangers of pigeon-holing people.

I doubt whether my questioner could have foreseen what his or her question provoked in me, and I hope that he or she does not mind me using the question as a launch pad for discussion, but I feel strongly about the issues involved. If he or she considers my reply to be a good all-round one, then I would have succeeded in making my point.

29 Foodcourt for thought

When I was first asked to write a piece for the 'Day in the life of. . .' column in the BAC journal *Counselling*, my first inclination was to decline. After all, I don't have a typical day, nor do I work full-time as a counsellor. I have a varied working life. However, although my appointment is an academic one, I do see clients regularly and am actively involved in the training and supervision of counsellors. So, on further reflection, I decided to accept the invitation.

I want to share with you an experience which I frequently seek out that, despite its apparently mundane quality, is important to me in that it helps to sustain me in the aforementioned activities. I want to write about the time I spend in the passenger lounge of the Foodcourt at Euston Station. As regularly as possible, I head for this haven (a term I use advisedly) placed as it is in the midst of the hustle and bustle of city life. On busy days, I may spend only ten minutes there; however, when engagements are less pressing, I sit in the smoking section, sucking on my trusty Peterson pipe, sipping tea with extra milk (no sugar) for anything up to two hours. What draws me to this place?

First, odd as it may seem, I have always found being alone when all around me is full of activity immensely soothing. It reflects a perverse side of my character to be going nowhere when everyone else is on the move. I find that I can think with greater clarity under such conditions. So, at the beginning of the day, if my schedule permits, I take the Watford line from Queen's Park to Euston and sit in 'my' section of the Foodcourt, preparing myself for the rigours of the day. Similarly, after work, whenever I can, I head for my sanctuary to process the day's events, allowing my thoughts free rein and generally winding down from the intensity of being with people where the focus of such encounters is on dealing with pain and doubt: the pain of clients

---

First published in 1992.

struggling to be themselves and the doubt of trainee counsellors struggling to become effective helpers.

At other times, when not so pressed for time, I head for Euston Station either to think or to write. There are just too many interruptions at work for me to get any creative work done and my study at home is now too much like a library to provide the urgency that I need to think productively. In contrast, the bustle of Euston station and the calm that I can generate for myself within that bustle is, for me, a powerful catalyst for innovation. Thus, I have conceived many book projects there, as well as ideas for new training courses. Last year, for example, when I was told to devise a more 'cost-effective' version of the MSc in Counselling that I direct at Goldsmiths' College, I headed straight for the Foodcourt for inspiration and sustenance. Furthermore, when I need to write something within a short period of time, I take my portable word processor (the marvellous Tandy WP-2) off to Euston and, with a cup of tea by my side, I type away until the job is finished. Guess where I wrote this piece, for example?

So why Euston? Why not Charing Cross or Waterloo, which would both be far more convenient for me? Why do I feel so at home and at peace in the Foodcourt and so ill at ease at these other stations? At one level the answer is simple. Euston is warm. Try sitting in the concourse area at Waterloo station in winter and you'll probably freeze. Try to find a comfortable seat anywhere at Charing Cross. However, the truth is a little more complex. Aside from physical comfort, the fact that one can travel to Birmingham from Euston has an important role to play here.

When I was unemployed in Birmingham from 1983 to 1985, I had occasion to travel to London Euston (as the train announcers call it) on various fruitless missions. Being a Londoner and very nostalgic, I had a sense that I was coming home on these journeys and found this quite comforting. I think that I re-experience some of that comfort whenever I sit in the Foodcourt.

Although I have stressed the solitary nature of this experience, I do appreciate seeing a friendly face. So, if you ever pass the Foodcourt at Euston Station, look in the passenger lounge and if you see a small balding figure smoking a Peterson pipe, lost in thought or tapping away on a portable word processor, do say hello and join me for a cup of tea. I take mine with extra milk, no sugar!

30 A note on how I used RET to overcome my emotional problems

When I was about four, I developed a stammer which led to a long and persistent period of teasing by my schoolmates in primary and secondary school. As a result, I began to view myself as a bit of a freak which, not surprisingly, hardly helped me to overcome my speech problem. I was taken (and in some instances dragged) to a variety of speech therapists over the ensuing years who uniformly failed to help me one iota with my stammer. I began to withdraw from talking in public, loathed speaking on the telephone and would literally quake with fear if anybody asked me my surname – which at the time was 'Denbin'* because I would give a good impression of a machine gun being fired while trying to pronounce it. I did not have a clear idea of the 'cause' of my anxiety, believing wrongly that the prospect of stammering was the main determinant rather than the 'awfulness' of such a prospect. In my teens, I went to a local elocution teacher who taught me how to speak on the breath and this helped quite a bit, although I was still anxious about speaking in public. It was only when I reached my early twenties that I got my first real help in overcoming my speech anxiety. This came when I saw Michael Bentine on television relating how he overcame his stammering problem. He told himself 'If I stammer, I stammer, too bad', or a similar variant. This seemed eminently sensible to me and I resolved to try this, albeit replacing his 'too bad' with my more evocative 'fuck it!'. I simultaneously came to the conclusion that I had, up to that point, been defining myself as a 'stammerer', which of course, was an over-generalisation. I undertook to re-define myself as a person who stammered at times, who spoke fluently at other times and who did a thousand and one other things too. With these cognitive techniques, I helped myself to a great extent,

---

First published in 1990.

*I changed my name from David Denbin to Windy Dryden mainly to avoid feelings of embarrassment concerning my difficulties in pronouncing 'Denbin'. I changed my first name to Windy because it was a nickname given me in my saxophone playing days, and because I liked it. Dryden was the name of our local telephone exchange.

particularly when I backed them up with a fair measure of in vivo exposure. I literally forced myself to speak up in various social situations while reminding myself that I could tolerate the discomfort of doing so. All these techniques, I subsequently discovered, are frequently employed in rational–emotive therapy (RET). I had, at that time, not heard of psychotherapy let alone RET. Using these techniques, I have, to date, nicely stammered (and more frequently spoken fluently) in various countries without anxiety and can now speak for an hour on local radio without much apprehension and free from anxiety. I achieved this largely as a result of my own efforts (with help from my elocution teacher) and enjoyed the fact that I was the major source of my own improvement.

In the mid-1970s, I trained as a counsellor, being schooled mainly in client-centred and psychoanalytical approaches. I entered therapy, at that time, partly because I thought it was a good idea for a trainee counsellor to be in 'personal therapy', but mainly because I was somewhat depressed. I had three relatively brief periods of psychoanalytical therapy with different practitioners. I found these experiences unhelpful in lifting my mood, was given no guidance on how to help myself and found most of the therapists' interventions puzzling, to say the least. One of my therapists slipped in, as it were, some psychodramatic techniques which helped me to 'see' that my problem basically involved feelings of inadequacy. These were unfortunately traced back to my childhood which distracted me from solving my mood problem. I decided at the end of my third unsuccessful therapy that enough was enough and that I'd better help myself as best I could. I turned to Ellis and Harper's (1975) book *A New Guide To Rational Living* because it stressed the use of self-help methods and because its content reminded me of my own successful efforts at overcoming my speech anxiety. I resolved to stop putting myself down, to accept myself as a fallible human being no matter what, and again pushed myself to do a number of things I wanted to do but was scared of doing because of the perceived threat to my 'fragile ego'. My depression lifted rather quickly and I began to feel more alive. All this without delving into my 'sacred' childhood.

I remembered, at this time, that my clients had, from the beginning of my counselling career, asked for more specific help than I was providing them through my reflections, clarifications and interpretations. I resolved to get trained in RET, believing then, as I do now, that it is essential to be trained in counselling methods before using them with clients. This I did and I noted that (1) the large majority of my clients liked my new, more active–directive counselling approach, and (2) I felt more congruent practising RET. I seemed to have found my theoretical and practical counselling niche.

Since then, I have continued to use RET on myself. I have employed rational–emotive methods to overcome my anxiety about making an important career decision. I decided, as a result, to leave my full-time tenured academic position at Aston University, taking 'voluntary' redundancy. Unfortunately, I overestimated my employability and was unemployed for two years, during which time I coped with my new status with disappointment but did not make myself depressed. During the two-year period I applied for and was rejected for 54 jobs or new positions. RET helped me in particular to overcome my anger about being turned down for retraining as a clinical psychologist. On being rejected, I began to believe such self-defeating ideas as 'How dare they refuse ME. Who do they think they are? They should accept such a fine fellow and a scholar as myself and one with such good credentials to boot!'. Noting that I was angry, I first accepted myself for needlessly angering myself and then disputed my irrational ideas. 'Why shouldn't these people have their own [albeit, in my view, misguided] opinions which led them to reject me?' The answer, in both cases, was the same: NO DAMNED REASON. I reminded myself that, whilst I considered them to be wrong, they don't have to be right, and they are obviously right from their perspective. I'm still annoyed about their decisions whenever I think about it – but am not angry.

I have, thus, gained more therapeutic benefit from my own rationale–motive self-help methods than from formal therapy. Consequently I believe that my preferred therapy orientation – RET – reflects both my decided preference for helping myself in my own life and my view that therapists do better when they directly aid clients to help themselves in their lives. RET nicely succeeds, for me, in both respects.

Index

accreditation, 74–75
adherence criterion, in research, 77–78
advertising, of training courses, 53–55
anger, and RET, 101
'appropriate', loose use of, 33
'around', loose use of, 33–34
assignments, between-session, 14
Aston University counselling course, 88–89
attitudes, dysfunctional, 3
audio tapes, 13–17
    clients' response to, 17
    and confidentiality, 16
    in counselling, 13–15
    security of, 15
    in supervision, 15–16
'authentic chameleon' (Lazarus), 28
'automatic thoughts', 3

BAC see British Association for Counselling
Beck, Aaron, 2
behaviour therapy, 11
    see also cognitive–behavioural approach
beliefs see irrational beliefs, rational beliefs
Bentine, Michael, 99
'bespoke tailor' (therapeutic), 27–29
bonds (therapeutic), 4, 5
Bordin, Ed, 4
British Association for Counselling, 74
    Courses Recognition Group, 74, 83
bumping into clients, 66–68

case material
    confidentiality of published, 48–49
    press disclosure of, 50–52
    WD's, 58–65
change see therapeutic change
'change-related' task domain, 5–6
clarity of communication, 32
clients
    bumping into, 66–68
    courage of, 42
    developing confidence in, 41–42
    'expectations' of, 32–33
    fear of, 42
    and outcome, 81, 82

    risk–taking by, 42
    uniqueness of, 23
code of ethics, 6, 49
    see also confidentiality; ethical issues
cognitive therapy, 2–3
    compared with RET, 3
    for stammering (self-help), 99
cognitive–behavioural approach, 2–3, 4, 36
    see also behaviour therapy; cognitive
        therapy; rational–emotive therapy
confidence, developing client, 41–42
confidentiality
    audio tapes and, 16
    and the press, 50–52
    of published case material, 48–49
core conditions, 5, 10–11
counselling
    audio tape procedures in, 13–17 passim
    behaviour therapy, 11, 36–37
    cognitive–behavioural approaches, 2–3,
        4, 36–37
    disparaging remarks between
        approaches, 35–37
    'Drydenisation' of, 93
    humanistic–existential approach, 4
    integrative approaches, 29
    non-directive, 7–9
    person-centred, 7, 36
    psychodynamic approach, 4, 11, 36
    style, 5
    telephone, 46
    see also counselling relationship; coun-
        sellors; literature; rational–
        emotive therapy; research; skills;
        techniques
counselling relationship
    quality of the, 5, 10, 12
    see also therapeutic alliance; therapeutic
        relationship
counsellor(s)
    dilemmas, 58–62
    discomfort of, 22–23
    finding a, 24–25
    flexibility of, 21, 27–29
    interpersonal style of, 5

counsellor(s) (contd)
    personal therapy for, vi, 80–82
    register of, 52, 75
    see also accreditation; counselling; train-
        ing; training courses
countertransference, negative, 80
Courses Recognition Group (BAC), 74, 83

damning, 3
Davies, P.G.K., 46–47
Diana, Princess, 50–51
directiveness, 8–9
disparaging remarks between approaches,
    35–37
Dryden *see* Windy Dryden
'Drydenisation' of counselling, 93

eclectic approach, 37
    see also integrative approaches
education, vs 'training', 70–73
Ellis, Albert, 3, 10–12 *passim*, 38
    in the 'Gloria' interview, 10, 12
ethical issues
    in counselling research, 46
    see also code of ethics, confidentiality
exaggerated evaluations, 3
'expectation', loose use of, 32–33

Feel the Fear and do it Anyway, 42
Feltham, Colin, 93
flexibility
    clinical, v
    counsellor, 21, 27–29
frustration tolerance, low, 3

Gammage, Philip, 72
'Gloria' interview/video, 10–12 *passim*
goals (therapeutic), 4, 5

humanistic–existential approach, 4

insurance, professional indemnity, 63–65
integrative approaches, 29
    see also eclectic approach
'Interpersonal Process Recall' (Kagan), 16
interventions, counsellor, 21, 22
irrational beliefs, 3, 38–40 *passim*
    see also rational beliefs

Jeffers, Susan, 42

Kagan, Norman, 16
Kopp, Sheldon, 9

Lambert, M.J., 72
Lancaster University Student Counselling
    Service, 91
language, imprecise use of, 32
Lazarus, Arnold, 28
limits of therapy, 61
literature on counselling, 46
low frustration tolerance, 3

methodology, research, 76–79
    see also research
multimodal perspective, 28
'musts', 3

Nelson-Jones, Richard, 21
New Guide to Rational Living (Ellis and
    Harper), 100
non-directive counselling, 7–9
Norcross, John, 81

outcome, client, 81, 82

'person-centred' approach, 7, 36
personal therapy
    for counsellors, vi, 80–82
    practice-focused, 82
    WD's, 100
Postgraduate Diploma in Counselling and
    Educational Settings (University of
    Aston), 88–89
press (the), disclosure of case material,
    50–52
professional indemnity insurance, 63–65
'professional' tasks, 6
psychoanalytic approach, 36
psychodynamic approach, 4, 11
    see also psychoanalytic approach
psychotherapy *see* counselling; personal
    therapy; therapy
publishing activities (WD's), 93–94

questions, open vs closed, 15

rational beliefs, 39
    see also irrational beliefs
rational–emotive therapy (RET), 2, 3, 14
    anger and, 101
    compared with cognitive therapy, 3
    criticisms of, 36–37
    therapeutic relationship in, 10–12
    WD's personal use of, 91, 99–101
rationality
    misrepresentation of, 39–40
    semantics of, 38–40
    see also irrational beliefs; rational beliefs
register of counsellors/therapists, 52, 75
    relationship *see* counselling relation-
        ship; therapeutic alliance; thera-
        peutic relationship
research, 76–79
    adherence criterion in, 77
    on counsellors' personal therapy, 81
    'differentiability' in, 78
    ethical issues in, 46
    literature, 46
    'purity' in, 78
    'quality' in, 78–79
response prevention, 22–23
risk-taking, client, 42
Rogers, Carl, 7, 9, 13

Schon, D.A., 71
self-defeating patterns, 41
shadchonim, 25–26
'shoulds', 3
skills
    courses in counselling, 83–85
    see also techniques
staff:student ratios, on skills courses, 85
stammering (WD), 99–100
Stein, D.M., 72
supervision, 6
    use of audio tapes in, 15–16

tapes see audio tapes
tasks (therapeutic), 4–6 *passim*
    'change–related' task domain, 5–6
    'professional', 6
techniques, 28
    see also skills
telephone counselling, 46
therapeutic alliance, v–vi, 4–6
    bonds, 4, 5
    goals, 4, 5
    tasks, 4–6 *passim*
    see also counselling relationship; thera-
        peutic relationship
therapeutic change, obstacles to, 41–43
therapeutic relationship
    neglecting the, 10–12
    in RET, 10–12 *passim*
    Therapy Relationship Questionnaire, 11
    see also counselling relationship; thera-
        peutic alliance
therapy
    limits of, 61
    see also counselling; personal therapy

Therapy Relationship Questionnaire
    (Truax and Carkhuff), 11
training
    in counselling skills, 83–85
    vs 'education', 70–73
    importance of personal therapy in,
        80–82
    see also accreditation; training courses
training courses
    advertising of, 53–55
    Aston University, Dept of Educational
        Enquiry, 88–89
    BAC Courses Recognition Group, 74, 83
    in counselling skills, 83–85
    staff:student ratios in, 85
    see also training

UK Standing Conference on Psychotherapy,
    74–75
    register of therapists, 75

warmth, counsellor, 11
Windy Dryden
    bumping into a client, 66–68
    case material, 58–65
    'Day in the life of...', 97–98
    'Drydenisation' of counselling, 93
    experience of redundancy, 88–92
    job applications/interviews, 90–92
        passim, 95
    personal therapy, 100
    personal use of RET, 91, 99–101
    professional self-view of, 96
    publishing activities of, 93–94
    as RET practitioner, 100